THE CANARY

THE CANARY

A Journey through Psychosis

JEFF MALDEREZ

Jeff Malderez Artist

Contents

bio.site/jeffmalderez

*A handwritten, non- A.I. generated, manuscript.

First published 2010. Jeff Malderez, Chipmunka Publishing.

Second Edition 2014. Jeff Malderez, CreateSpace.

Third Edition 2024. Jeff Malderez, IngramSpark.

ISBN: 979-8-9909273-0-8

Jeff Malderez was born in 1978 in Aurillac, France and, after having lived abroad most of his life, went to university in 1997 to study psychology. In 2000, he started experiencing severe panic attacks and the onset of acute 'psychosis'. This journey took him through many mystical and spiritual adventures throughout the city where he lived and, more importantly, in his mind and being. Not only does Jeff have a BSc in psychology and two post graduate certificates: one in mental health art group facilitation and another in psychological therapies, but he has also worked in the adult mental health field in England and now as a Peer Counselor in the USA.

He wishes to publish this book, his first publication, for the benefit of others undergoing similar experiences and to help them reframe their experiences into a more helpful and ultimately, he hopes, a more meaningful framework. Appealing not only to this group of people but also to academics, professionals and the wider public, he hopes that *The Canary: A Journey Through Psychosis* can help de-stigmatize the nature of 'psychosis' and help to dispel some of the myths surrounding it. *Please note*: some strong language is used as well as drug and alcohol use is described in this book.

For Jeremy H.

Thank-you so much for being my friend...
and for seeing the magic where others could not.

I also want to say a big thank-you to both Reverend Andrew Atkins for writing the foreword to this book and to Dr. David Lukoff for his wonderful endorsement.

Endorsement by Dr. David Lukoff

Like Jeff, I also underwent a spiritual emergency which temporarily impaired my ability to function in consensual reality and everyday social life. Luckily, I was able see the experience through to a positive resolution with the support of my friends and family, obviating the need for traditional medical intervention such as hospitalization or medication.

Yet since becoming a licensed psychologist, I have often found myself face-to-face with individuals in the same state of consciousness that Jeff and I had been in: convinced that they were reincarnations of great spiritual figures, reporting communication with religious figures, believing they had a messianic mission to save the world etc.

I think accounts such as Jeff's can help sensitize both the culture and the mental health professions to recognize when people are having a temporary spiritual emergence episode so that they won't be hauled off to a hospital when much less restrictive approaches would achieve the same or even better outcomes.

I applaud Jeff's courage in getting this out into the world.

David Lukoff, PhD Professor of Psychology
Institute of Transpersonal Psychology
Founder, Spiritual Competency Resource Center

Foreword by Rev. Andrew Atkins

HELLO there! Now, I may be wrong, but I reckon you're at the foreword page for one of three reasons.

1. You are thinking of buying 'The Canary' and you hope that this might help your decision. Please read on, I'll try to help you make that decision.
2. You are wondering whether to skip straight to chapter one coz this might be long and irrelevant, or maybe it will be worth a read? It will be brief, I hope relevant, but I'll leave you to decide on the worthiness!
3. You always read the foreword to your purchases. Hey, I'm impressed, let's get on with it.

When Jeff asked me to read his book and write this foreword for him I have to say that I was both moved and, if I'm honest, a little daunted. I read the book, or at least tried to from at least four different angles. As a parent, which I am. As the minister who has played a small part in Jeff's journey. As, I hope, a new friend of Jeff's. And finally, as someone who knows very little, if indeed anything about mental health.

Once in a while a book comes along that you pick up and begin reading completely unaware that the hardest thing you will have to do next in your life is put it back down. 'The Canary' is one such book. I could physically feel myself being pulled into its pages to share in Jeff's journey. Jeff's writing enabled me to know the characters, and himself, in such depth that I wanted to read it in one go, but that would have been a VERY BIG mistake indeed! Why? Because I would have missed out on so much more.

'The Canary' is disturbing yet warming, alarming yet full of hope, shocking yet touching...oh I could go on and on, but over all this is a book that needs to be read, that demands to be read. It is a book that I am convinced will pull you into its pages. But heed my warning, read it too quickly or only once at your own loss.

As a parent, minister, friend and human being I am more aware, more understanding, more open minded and a great deal richer for experiencing 'The Canary'.

If you are anything like me then this book will move you, it will reshape you, it will challenge you, it will make you laugh, it will make you cry, but I am certain that like me, you will be a richer and more rounded person because of it.

So go on, turn the page now to Chapter 1. Foreword over!

Reverend Andrew Atkins

Dark Angels

You are troubled by your dark angels...
You seek to tame their wildness...
But they are the potential source of creativity within you...
If you deny them, banish them, seek to destroy them, they will drain you of
passion as they retreat,
and you will become pale and lifeless...
And if they should return and storm your gates, you would then be destroyed...

However dark, they are still angels, guardians and protectors too...

Reverend Jim Cotter

I

Introduction

PART ONE: The Flight in...

When I got the news that I had been accepted to do an under-graduate degree in psychology at University, I could hardly wait to begin. Little did I know, however, that I was going to study it at a level far more intensely than I ever could have imagined. At the time it was a double celebration for me as my mother had also been offered a job at the same university. My brother was already studying at a university not so far away and so my mother and I moved up north in the autumn of 1997.

My first year went pretty much as one might expect. My keenness and motivation preceding the start of the course carried me pretty much most of the way through the year. I attended most lectures and enjoyed doing the essays I was required to do, particularly for my elective subject philosophy. I joined the gym and took full advantage of living in an area that had a busy social life. I got on well with my flatmates and made a few friends on my course. I passed the year fine with good marks overall.

The second year started pretty much as the first did. My flatmates and I were now living in a shared house and I was looking forward to the year, in particular my hypnosis module. Now being more acquainted with the local scene I began to establish a few contacts for the purpose of acquiring cannabis for those long nights essay writing and relaxing with mates. I had been 'introduced' to the powers of smoking this leaf back in the days when I was living abroad, while attending an international school in the city. At this stage, I would not have considered myself dependent on it; I simply enjoyed a smoke from time to time. However, I would say that I looked forward to the creative insights and thoughts that it gave me. As a result, during this time, I amassed a substantial amount of poetry, thoughts and theories on many aspects of life. It was an intensely creative time for me.

The first indication that something was definitely wrong came during my first final exam of that year. I was confident going into the exam room that I was well prepared and knew my stuff well. Upon receiving the paper I suddenly felt as though I could not sit there for two hours and write the exam. It was not that I did not feel able to answer the questions or simply had a memory block as it was all *there*, but for some reason I felt physically unable to do it. I began to sweat, shake and was unable to breathe properly. I forced myself to write half a page at which point all I could think was of getting out of there. That was it; I got up and left without looking back. After talking with my Mum about the incident, I could not be certain that it wouldn't happen again. I decided to go to my doctor for a sick note in order to be eligible for the re-takes in the summer. He prescribed some anti-anxiety drugs that had some adverse effects so I stopped taking them a few days later. Summer came and went. I sat the re-takes without a problem however.

The third and final year was to be, without a doubt, a major turning point. It was make or break as far as my degree was concerned and so the pressure was on. My housemates and I decided to move back into the same first year halls of residence, as living in private accommodation had taken its toll on our overdrafts. Within about a month of settling in we had made good friends with a flat of girls living on our floor and, indeed, myself and my flatmate Ben both developed close relationships with two of the girls from the same aforementioned flat. I couldn't have been happier. I thought I had finally found my soul mate in Josephine. She was the kind of person who honestly loved life; she was witty, outgoing, intelligent, and truly inspired me. I felt she encouraged the best out of me. I was alive when I was with her and before long we spent a considerable amount of time together, to the slight annoyance of both our mates no doubt. Talking with her was so easy and we often spent many a night chatting, writing poems, smoking and flirting. Time dissolved when with her; it soon became clear we had developed a very special bond.

Things progressed in that vein until one cold, windy day in early November. I had arranged to meet Josephine outside the students' union after lectures for lunch. Taking full advantage of the Sunday roast on offer, Jo and I piled our plates high. We paid and walked over to the smoking area to find a table. As usual, the place was packed. Eventually we sat at a table with only one other bloke on it. He was a quirky sort, slim, balding, shaven-haired, early forty's ish. He looked like a retro mature student with the facial qualities of a vulture, a bald head, piercing eyes and a pointy nose. Not the kind of guy you would like to meet in a dark side alley by the canal. Feeling somewhat uncomfortable, I felt the need to break the ice with this man so that I could have a more relaxing meal. "How are your roasties? Mine are a bit soggy..." I said. He slowly looked up and said "They're good. You must have had the last batch".

General introductory chit-chat followed. As it turned out, Steve had had quite a bit of business training as well as a great deal of experience in doing company projections. Upon hearing this, my ears pricked up, literally. Jo and I had talked at length of starting some kind of small business concerning my poetry, involving possibly performing and publishing it. Steve seemed very interested in my ideas and poetry and wished to hear more. He gave me his card and said that he would help me draw up a business plan, initially, seemingly free of charge. I came away from lunch with my head spinning with the possibilities. I was on a high of confidence and motivation.

2

Steve & Co.

About a week went by when I made the call to arrange to meet up with Steve again. He suggested that I came over to his place one day after uni as he didn't live far. On the way there it soon transpired that he lived in quite a notorious area for muggings and crime in general. Feeling somewhat anxious, I hurriedly made my way to his place as it was quickly getting dark.

"Jeff, what the fuck are you doin? You're going to a bloke's house who you've met only once. Man this ain't good, look at the houses and alleys – anyone could jump ya at any moment. Yeah ok – just shut up and walk quickly but like, as if you live here. Walk with confidence."

Once inside it soon became apparent that Steve was a man of taste, history and knowledge. Carved African sculptures were dotted around his living room, as were pages of the *Guardian*. A huge picture of a clown, done in a style similar to that of Jackson Pollack, hung on the wall. This unnerved me somewhat has I had always been afraid of clowns ever since I was young. Over a pot of tea, however, I settled down, showed him some of my poetry and we discussed possible avenues I could take with it. Suddenly, after putting on some music, he started skinning-up.

At which point he turned to me and asked whether I smoked. I replied that I did. The next few hours were filled with smoke, tea, tunes and chatter. As the time came for me to leave, Steve invited me to dinner in a few days' time when I could meet some of his friends, all of which, he thought I would get on well with.

Having checked that I could bring Jo along, we turned up at his place a few days later. Upon entering I was immediately hit by a curious mixture of smells. Dinner, apparently, was already a few hours into the making. Moroccan and Thai culinary influences were littered across the work surfaces with lemon grass, couscous, ginger and garlic all on display. Mixed into the aroma was also the faint but potent smell of a few hours of dope smoking. Standing in the living room, joint in hand, was Steve's friend Will. Looking a tad younger than myself, I felt pleasantly surprised as I feared a somewhat middle-aged gathering ahead with Jo and I sticking out like a sore thumb. Will had deferred from university for a few years in order to focus on developing his deejaying career. He was heavily involved in the underground mixing circle and regularly had gigs at venues throughout the city.

About half an hour later, two more of Steve's friends arrived. Vince and Jim were housemates living a few minutes away also in the same area. Both studying at the same University as me they had met Steve several months earlier and had become good friends with both Steve and Will. Jim was the typical dreadlocked philosophy student to the max; deep, laid back and one who seriously liked his weed. Vince, on the other hand, came from a well-to-do family from a shire somewhere north of London. He was outspoken, loud and seriously liked his clothes. Originally from Italy, we soon got on well, what with my family on my Dad's side being Spanish, both having the Mediterranean connection.

After having the time to chat and get to know each other we were then called to the table. To say that the meal was a banquet fit for a king would be a serious understatement. For starters, there were two starters. To begin with we had deep fried vegetables with a variety of dips and sauces followed by a light salad to clean the pallet. The main course consisted of a huge seafood paella dish with prawns, mussels, and shellfish all cooked with rice and a variety of oriental herbs and spices. Not really having the room for it I managed to eat a bit of the desert, chilli soaked vodka and Ben and Jerry's ice cream.

"This guy sure knows how to cook. Shame that Jo doesn't like seafood. Boy am I stuffed. I must remember to ask Will if I can copy his album...I like this track. I wish we could change the topic of conversation though. Student politics is as interesting as putting on a hat."

Over fresh filter coffee and spliffs we relaxed and digested for a few hours thereafter. It transpired that this kind of 'dinner' was not uncommon round at Steve's. In fact, it was more the norm Will assured me. Like my Dad, Steve took serious pride in his cooking and regarded it as one of his 'art forms'. With the amount of time and attention to detail I had observed being paid in the kitchen, this came as little surprise to me. I was beginning to think I could learn a lot from Steve and Co.

3

Finals

Going round to Steve's very quickly became a habit. In addition, my smoking habit also seemed to increase. As a result of the encouragement and extra source of inspiration I was getting my poetry folder soon turned from a thin pamphlet to a considerable volume of work. My notoriety as somewhat of a poet soon spread among the new group of friends I had made. Before long I was helping Will to put lyrics to his tracks and appeared on the university's radio station reciting some of my work for the Radical Ghanja Society. Soon after that I had my first performance reciting my work in front of an audience at one of the university's nightclubs.

"I hope Steve remembers to bring my performing hat. Damn it suits me – I should go to Peru or Chile, I would blend in quite nicely. Bloody hell Steve, where the hell are you? I go on in five minutes. Look at the size of the audience! Pathetic! Well Jeff, it is your first live gig – do you really want it to be packed? I s'pose not. There you are then! It will be good practice... and anyway here comes Steve – without the hat. Bloody typical."

Before I knew where I was my third year dissertation was due in and the finals were only a few days away. While I had spent a considerable amount of time devoted to 'study'; I often found myself thinking and composing more poetry. My thoughts were more focused around the need to create and be creative than on analysing, digesting and regurgitating material which bore less and less resemblance to actual human behaviour and psychology as I had experienced it. The fact I was not even allowed to do my third year project on the topic I wished, albeit with a considerable amount of justification and academic support and interest in the field, just dissuaded me further from what was 'asked' of me. I was beginning to seriously feel that university is not about thinking and questioning but about bums on seats and quashing any truly inspirational, and ultimately radical, ideas anyone had. "Where's the sodding progress?"

Jo, on the other hand, was a Godsend during this time. If it hadn't have been for her encouragement, cooking and revising with me I doubt I would have done a quarter of what I did.

Inevitably as the day of my first exam loomed both my family and myself became increasingly apprehensive as the events of last year's exams came flooding back. Walking into my first exam I felt nothing; absolutely nothing. No fear, no anxiety, no excitement, no anticipation, nothing. It was as if my body and senses were in the room but my heart and soul were elsewhere entirely. After beginning to write the first answer it was as if my hand and heart were completely disassociated. My hand knew the answer and was duly carrying out the motions in order to complete the question but my heart and soul couldn't care less. I finished the first exam in double quick time, however I did complete all the questions required.

As I faced the rest of the exams my hand was fighting a losing battle. My mind was stuck in the middle and while it had done enough to push my hand in the first exam it was by now siding with my heart and soul. By the end of my last exam I had had enough and walked out again half way through. Call it a major defense mechanism kicking into action or me simply giving up caring, I didn't know and quite simply didn't care. It was done and I felt as if a weight that had been built up over twenty-one years had been lifted. Never was I going to do that *ever* again.

"Well Jeff, what are you going to tell Mum, Jo and your mates about how your exams went? I'll say ok. You know you could've done better though don't you?! Yeah... and? What's your point? Go bug somebody else."

While my flatmates came back saying that they had done well or ok, I knew that they had all done fine. Implicitly, however, I knew that I was in 'trouble' as far as my degree was concerned but now there was nothing I could do, nor did I wish to. The last few weeks in the flats were weird and I felt as though I had already left uni the day I walked out of my last exam. I didn't go out 'celebrating' or go to the overpriced department ball. I knew this was causing tension and frustration for my flatmates and between Jo and myself, but all I wanted to do was leave.

4

www.E.com

As the summer rolled in I put my CV around town in the hope of finding some temporary work before making the 'big decision': what I wanted to do with the rest of my life. I already knew that I certainly wouldn't have the grades to go into psychology or psychiatry. I focused, instead, on data related jobs as I had already done several small contract jobs data entering and was keen to go into an Internet business. "Easy money, respectable job", I thought. A few weeks later, as I was expecting, I received an Ordinary degree in psychology. A smile spread across my face.

"Ordinary, eh? Who wants a poncy first-class degree with people thinking you're a pretentious, cocky, middle-class, up-start know-it-all anyway?! You once, Jeff. Yeah, well, I woke up...ordinary suits me fine. Never been 'ordinary' before – I like it. Yeah? Yes really."

Before long I was working full time for a small Internet entertainment company in town. Jo had gone back home for the summer and I was back living with my mother and brother. My Bro, like me, still had not made the big decision either and had already moved back the year before. When I wasn't working I spent almost all of my free time with

Steve and Co., either round at his place or going out for nature 'trips' with Jim and Vince as they often did.

Walking back from work one evening I received a text message:

It's not working out. Please let me go.

It was from Jo. She hadn't signed it or explicitly indicated that it was for me, but fear had already begun to set in. Still not quite believing it was meant for me I stopped at the nearest bar to get a drink. I double-checked the number to confirm that it was from her, it was. I always hated it when she went back home. On the phone she often sounded distant and I was always fearful that she would someday wonder why the hell she was with me rather than with any of her wittier and more successful bloke friends back home. I was also convinced her girlfriends disliked me and thought that I wasn't good enough for her. The sad truth of it was I also believed that. Several drinks and a phone call to my Dad later and it had still not sunk in fully.

Pissed, pissed-off and confused, all I could think was that I needed a smoke. Before long I was knocking at Steve's door. After telling Steve and Will, who was now staying at Steve's, what had happened they quickly started to point out the advantages of being single and how she wasn't right for me. I was still trying to get my head round how she did what she did with a text of all things, when the effects of the Jamaican Honey began to settle my mind and my racing heart. "Why don't you come out with us tonight?" Steve then asked. As it turned out, they were going to an underground dj gig in the north of the city and thought I could use a dance. For one that usually goes on the dance floor *only* after several pints, and given my recent piece of news, I thought me dancing would be highly unlikely. However, I didn't feel like going home and thought a few extra drinks was a good idea.

After having agreed, Steve than asked if I wished to partake in some of the white powder he was spreading out on the dining room table. I was so angry and hurt at this time that I did give it some thought, but decided to have another Jamaican Honey flavoured cone instead. Besides, the idea of shoving horse tranquilliser up my nose just simply didn't appeal to me.

"Why anyone prefers Ketamine to this luurvly Jamaican Honey is beyond me. Perhaps it's just amazing. Perhaps it's so good you just have to try it – once tried,

twice flied?...er... flown? What, Jeff? You're pissed and stoned and you've got work tomorrow. Oh sod work! Jo has just left me! I'm going out...and getting shit- faced! I think you already are. Yeah, well nice one..."

After all the drugs that were to be consumed that evening had been, and after Steve had changed into his African dancing robes, we made our way to the north of the city. Once inside it became clear that there were quite a number of people whom Steve and Will knew quite well, yet whom I had never met. Vince and Jim soon turned up and I wasted no time joining them with a pint. The venue was used for many things including events like this one. As such it was not your typical night-club. The evening, it seemed, had only been advertised through word of mouth and fliers distributed among friends. Everyone appeared to know everyone.

A while later Will came over to join us. After chatting to Jim, Will leaned over to me and said that he and the others were going to take a few pills and wondered if I wanted the half he had left over. By now the thought that I had ruined everything that I made for myself and for my life was plaguing me to such an extent that I couldn't think of anything else. "Any distraction would be better than this", I thought. With that I agreed and followed them to the toilets to take it. Will told me that it should take about half an hour to kick in and so I went for another drink.

About forty-five minutes later the first dj was already on stage doing his set. I was beginning to think that I had probably smoked too much earlier and it was counter- balancing the effect of the pill. Suddenly Steve took to the dance floor and started dancing solo with all his heart. For some strange reason I felt that he needed me to join him. While I had drunk quite a lot by now I still would never have been the only other one on the floor. I didn't care, however. I shot up from the table and ran to join him going into full dance-mode upon hitting floor. I made my way over to Steve who appeared to be completely unaware of his surroundings; his attention totally dedicated to his dancing and

the music. When he did finally open his eyes and saw me moving haphazardly in front of him he smiled knowingly then closed his eyes again.

"What's up doc? Why are you ignoring me now? Actually I don't care. What a tune!! Gotta get Will here! ...oh there you are! When did you come over? Move those legs Jeff! Yeah!! This tunes' going right through me – I ain't dancing, I'm just riding on the sound waves...I'm surfin!"

By now, when I did opened my eyes, I could make out about ten of us were surfin' on the dance floor. The waves were getting bigger and bigger as the set continued. Each tune was a new challenge to me and I just couldn't stop. I seemed to be moving faster and faster, and higher and higher over the waves.

"I'm so not on the dance floor now!! Boy I love this...this is truly amazing! Yeah – I bet I could do anything now!! Find out, find out Jeff! Hay you! "Can you fly on this? Will you teach me? Please?!" God you're so kind ...and gorgeous, thank-you. Have a kiss: *smack* ...God I love this!"

I danced for well over an hour when Will came up to me. He told me to make sure that I drink a lot of water and often, then handed me a bottle. The rest of evening I spent dancing with Will, Vince, Jim and their housemates. I felt like a kid again without any cares in the world. The brake-up was by now a distant memory. I was so sad when the house lights came up that when Steve asked if I wanted to come back to his for a coffee and smoke I quickly agreed. By now it was well past two o'clock and so I asked Steve if I could kip on his sofa. He thought it was good idea.

I was woken early by Will in accordance to my request given the night before, although I had no memory of that. Time for work. I hadn't slept long but I shot up with bags of

energy still left over from the night before. Walking through town I felt like dancing several times but resisted. I stopped off to get some chewing gum. For some reason I just felt like chewing although I wasn't hungry. Once inside the office floor I floated past others already at their keyboards with their sad, dreary Monday-looking faces.

Suddenly I caught a glimpse of a screen-saver on someone's monitor. It was the same green bits of information cascading down as in the film *The Matrix*. To this day I still cannot fully describe or understand what happened next. I glanced down at my feet treading the floor in front of me and then at my hands. Everything, everywhere, had suddenly morphed into the same green bytes and bits. It wasn't simply an after image of the monitor's image as it lasted far too long for that. Moreover, everything not only looked like *The Matrix*, but I could also understand and *feel* how everything interacted with each other at the same time. I felt like I was not only walking towards my office, but *was* also the table with the keyboards and monitors sitting on me, *was* the door attached to the walls as well as the pen my colleague was writing with. I have no words or thoughts to describe the experience, as there were none. I simply knew and felt it.

By the time it came to finish for the day my packet of chewing gum had nearly all gone. While I had had several pieces throughout the day, I had also given a great many away also. I suddenly remembered what Will had told me the night before about how people on E very frequently chew gum and often too. In that split second the behaviour of most of my colleagues in the office suddenly became amazing clear to me. Those people chewing gum were the ones I thought were the most in their own worlds. They seemed very blasé about what they were doing; yet very focused at the same time. They couldn't sit still, often blasting into spontaneous song and making endless cups of tea. From then on I was absolutely certain that at least four out of the six people in the room with me were on E most of the time, including my supervisor.

5

The Pilgrimage

Before meeting Steve and Co. I had been fairly naïve as to the full extent and nature of the underground drug culture in this country. Having left England in 1987 when I was nine, I was either too young or had missed out on all the acid parties, Second Summer of Love and the rave phenomenon. No bad thing I suspect, but it did leave me very out of touch with people around my own age.

For a while now Steve and Will had been working at putting a night on at the same venue in the north of the city. Will had become quite an accomplished music producer, working endlessly on Steve's computer and the various sound software packages installed. Believing in his talent and ability as an artist, Steve was financially backing the event dubbed *The Pilgrimage*. There was a lot riding on this event for both of them.

As the big night drew closer I got more and more involved in the project. Up until the very day it was to kick-off I was distributing flyers around my old student residence and putting up the odd poster here and there. They wanted a lot of people to be there in order to make a good return on Steve's investment. I certainly began to appreciate how much organisation and effort went in to putting on such a night. Apart from the actual creation and technical side of the music, the hiring of the venue and bouncers, the insurance, the lighting equipment, and publicity all had to be dealt with. It was a unique learning experience for me.

Sometime that day my Grandma called me expressing a concern she and my Mum had about who I was spending most of my time with. She then cautiously asked me if I had got involved with some kind of sect or cult. While I was shocked at this suggestion, I nevertheless understood the reasons behind it. I assured her that I had not gotten involved in anything like that and did my best to alleviate her concerns.

I arrived a few hours early that evening to help set up. Most of this time, however, I spent helping to suspend the biggest army mesh camouflage net I had ever seen above the dance floor. As the punters started to stroll in, albeit in twos and threes to begin with, Steve asked me if I could 'man' the cloakroom. I was a little disappointed at this, but as it wouldn't get going for a while yet I thought that when it did I could easily pass the baton so-to-speak. An hour after the official starting time the head count was only about twenty. I could sense that Steve was beginning to get a bit edgy, so I stayed out of his way.

I started to strike up a conversation with the man sitting next to me by the cloakroom. I had met him once before at an underground dj gig at a shady pub a few weeks before. One could only describe him as quite a 'character'. He looked about sixty-odd, with a white mane and beard. He was a regular to events like these, I was told, and was known only as 'Magic Murry'. During our first conversation I realised that there was very little in this world Magic Murry had not seen, done or experienced, and always had a pack of Murry mints with him. Hence his name, I surmised. As such he possessed an air of wisdom about him, just like Gandalf in *The Lord of the Rings*. On the dance floor, however, his wisdom quickly gave way to delight. His 'dancing' could only be described as being similar to that of an imp-like creature jumping about on hot coals. It was such a joyful, heart-warming sight, however, that I doubt I shall ever forget it. This in mind, I really hoped he would be going on the dance floor that night. I somehow knew I would get my wish.

A while later and the head count had increased considerably. Thinking that hardly anyone else would be turning up I left the cloakroom to find Will. He was due on soon as the first dj was beginning to finish his set. I found him backstage, joint in hand as usual. As the bouncers were friends of Steve's, smoking was permitted if done discreetly. After sharing a few joints that were being passed around I asked Will for the pill I had arranged for earlier that day. I took it quickly. I had every intention of doing some major surfin' that evening, especially with Will's music. I couldn't wait.

As Will came on he received a rapturous applause. I didn't know if it was because he was wearing a policeman's helmet or because he had a lot of friends on the dance floor.

"Must be both", I thought. As the first track kicked in I immediately recognised it and went straight into surfin'-mode. It was as if the music was a catalyst for the effects of the pill. I was right at the front of the dance floor with Vince, Jim and the rest of their housemates. By now Steve seemed to have relaxed and had joined us at the front in his traditional, trademark, dancing robes.

*"Yeah, now we're surfin'! God I love this!! Will's hat looks like a wizard's hat now!...weird. Hey, speaking of wizard, where's Magic Murry? I hope he's still here. Go find 'im Jeff! Excuse me...sorry, just passin'...oh hiya – gotta give you a hug later! *wink*...excuse me...There he is! *smile* Still the same 'ole Muz! Man those coals must be hot tonight – look how high he's goin!!"*

I surfed with Magic Muz for a while and then asked him if he wanted to join us at the front. He declined and added "You go back and join your friends laddy!" After about an hour of surfin' back at the front I went for another bottle of water. At the bar stood a scruffy, Manc-looking young man as rigid as a poll. Feeling in a very chatty mood all of a sudden I quickly tried to strike up a bit of conversation. "How come you ain't dancing? The music's amazing on the floor!" "I'm not here for the music", he said, "I'm just here to settle a score with that fucker on stage." "Oh, right..." I mumbled as I made a b-line straight for the bouncer. I outlined the situation to him and told him to grab the Manc if he went anywhere near Will.

I also found Steve and told him about the Manc's intentions. After asking me to point him out he told me that Will had made some enemies in his time, and said to leave it with him. I saw Steve speaking with the Manc sometime later who quickly left thereafter. As it turned out Steve had slipped him some dope. Will had apparently encroached on his territory and he was out for payback. To this day I have no idea what Steve had said to him or why he was so quick to leave. Anyway, the score appeared to have been settled.

After that I wasted no more time and headed back for the dance floor. As Will was reaching the high point of his set, the strobe lights and smoke machine kicked-in. The sight was truly awesome at this point. The effects of both the pill and the smoke made the later seem like real ocean waves, with the music acting as the current. I got more and more into my dancing and loved every minute.

At one point while not really noticing the crowd, with my body surfin' and my mind racing, I suddenly spun round faster and faster. What prompted me to do this I had no idea. But the realisation that followed shocked and excited me to such an extent that I felt like I had finally reached the end of some kind of initiation. It was quick and felt extremely profound.

"Spin, spin, spin...! The African shaman...Will the wizard...Magic Muz...the flying girl...Why isn't anyone saying anything?...the music Jeff! It's respect for the music! They all know, they all know why they're here. They aren't social-ising – they're meeting up again – in this place. In the waves, in the currents, it's a different reality man. No one knows it's here until they get here – and then they stay! A real utopia in suburbia!

Spin...spin...Look Jeff, look at everyone! They all have the same expression on their face! Even the bouncers! Jeff! It's a club man! It's a secret society!! The initiation is the pill and the surfin'! Look at the respect between them. See how much room they give Muz and Steve – they must be high up in the group's hierarchy! It's so simple, so obvious now!...and you've finally made it!!! Welcome to the club Jeff!!"

I can only describe the feeling I had at that moment to the dis-covery a twelve year-old boy has when he is playing 'down stairs' and has his first orgasm - times a hundred. You have absolutely no idea it was there, or possible, or that euphoric, until it happens. In a split second everything becomes amazingly clear. All the talk, innuendoes, looks and behaviour that once seemed so alien suddenly becomes so transparent. Yet this was very different for a variety of reasons. Firstly, once I 'broke through' I stayed there all evening. There was also the hierarchical structure, which I had implicitly felt existed but did not understand. Now I understood it and what was more, I was a part of it. Lastly, and most importantly, it was like stepping onto another plane of reality. Words woefully fail to even scrape the surface of what I mean now. Those of you reading this who have been there will understand. Yes, it was a chemical change in my brain and body activity. However, it was also a change in perception, spirit, and being.

As the evening was drawing to a close, I began to believe that the name of the event was in no way a coincidence. I had been on a long journey of discovery and now I had reached my destination. Unlike the end of the other night I slowly, this time, made my way over to

Steve. I waited for him to say his good-byes and got his attention. "I'm there now. Thank-you so much!" I said respectfully and beaming with gratitude. "I'm so pleased you're finally with us Jeff, but boy have you taken your time!" he said with a smile and a hug. For a few minutes we chatted about my realisation 'moment' and the observations I had made. He was particularly interested in the comparison I made with Muz and him as high-raking shamans or teachers within the 'circle'. In response to his comparison, however, he simply replied "I just know a thing or two. That's all." I knew, however, that I had hit the nail on the head and that he was just being modest.

From that night onwards Steve and Co.'s behaviour towards me changed immensely, yet subtly. Before *The Pilgrimage*, I had always felt that they interacted with me in the same way a teacher would with a child. Not patronising but educating. There after it seemed I had learned all the lessons they had to teach me. I had now also become a teacher, an equal among the waves of my fellow surfers. And I loved it.

6

Moving Out

That was it. I was not going to waste a single minute of my life from then on. Things were going to change. The first day back at work I went straight into the boss's office and asked to speak with him. He was a self-made millionaire entrepreneur. The website I was working on was only one of many little hobbies for him, created for the sole purpose of making more money. While he was charming and had the gift of the gab, he was also your archetypal capitalist. He was a Thatcherite; hell bent on the acquisition of money at the expense of the needs and conditions of his workers. Even before *The Pilgrimage*, I was unhappy at work. There was no respect, no genuine concern for colleagues and an office atmosphere you could cut a knife with.

I wasn't prepared to put up with it any longer. I explained that while I had been on my probationary period, *I* had concluded that the *company* wasn't good enough for me and would like to resign forthwith. He was a little taken aback when I said this and asked me for my reasons. I simply replied "I now realise that there is more to life than the acquisition of money, and as such I'm going to pursue a career that fulfils me more." He asked me to reconsider but I said that my mind was made up.

"If I didn't dislike you so much I would actually feel sorry for you pal. You have absolutely no idea why we're here and what's ultimately important in life. Have ya? No, I could be talking Thai for all it matters. I'm not even going to try to explain it to you. No, you go back to making money in your dingy office feeling proud of yourself. I'm going outside in the sunshine ... lie on the grass, relax, experience, and live. Adios..."

With that I left his office, said goodbye to the others, picked up my coat and strolled out of there with my head held high and a smile beaming across my face. I soon met up with Vince and Jim and told them what had happened. They were pleased for me and both gave me a hug. For the rest of the day we spent it in the sunshine, smoking, and being in nature. When the day drew to a close the time had come to face the music back at home. I knew that my mother and brother would be worried that I had quit my job, so I had to convince them it was the right move for me.

"Jeff, just go in there and tell them the truth. You have finally woken up to the delight of nature and reality and you cannot do a job which will separate you from that. Without the sunlight and nature you will die, if not physically but mentally and spiritually. Yea ok, that sounds good. Ok here goes nothing..."

In I walked. Mum was in the kitchen preparing dinner and my Bro was watching TV. "Did you have a good day?" my Mum asked. "Yes – a great day – in fact so good that I decided to quit my job" I said with conviction. My mother's face then dropped and the wrinkles appeared around her eyes like they normally do when she is very worried about something. I could sense that she was very disappointed in me and was beginning to worry. "Why on Earth did you do that?" she then asked. "Because I had had enough of staring at that bloody monitor all day – especially on a day like today – look at the light and clouds – there is where I want to be – not stuck in a dingy office all day" I replied.

The next question then came from out of the blue. "Are you on drugs?" I didn't see the relevance or importance of this question – especially not when faced with the very real and deep feeling I had and had discovered about myself and nature. "That's fucking irrelevant and trivial and quite frankly insulting, it's purely missing the whole point Mum!" I thought. Instead of saying all of that to her, I simply replied "No" and left it at that. Even my Bro joined in and asked me "What the hell are you on?"

"I have to get out of here – they don't understand me at all – call Vince Jeff – that's it I'm moving into their place. Fuck it."

With that I went straight upstairs and started packing. I could hear Mum talking to my Bro in muffled voices downstairs, but I didn't care in the least. I called Vince on my mobie and told him about what had happened. He then told me that they had a spare room in their house and they would be delighted to have me as their housemate. That was it, he was on his way with Jim to collect me and I couldn't have been happier.

After packing a few clothes into an old sports bag I came downstairs to face the music once again. Mum was standing at the bottom of the stairs. "Here it comes again" I thought. "What are you going to live on?" she blurted out, half in anger and half in desperation no doubt I thought.

"Jeff, this is your last chance to explain it to her. If you can. But Jeff, what kind of a fucking question is that? Look, you know that the kind of love, life and reality you are in now you can survive anything – so tell her. Make her understand that. But how Jeff? Well..."

"I will live on love" I replied and carried on walking down the stairs. The rest of the 'conversation' was like a muffled blur for me as I tried my best to tune her and my Bro out until Vince and Jim came to collect me. It wasn't long until they turned up outside. Thank God!

7

Withnail & I & Us

When we got back to the house the others were there to greet me. They were all delighted with the news of me moving in and so was I. We hadn't discussed rent or council tax or anything like that, I would get another job soon, I thought, and it will sort itself out. To celebrate, Vince and Jim suggested another nature 'trip' that weekend to the Lake District. Vince had got his hands on the address of Monty's 'country retreat' in the film *Withnail & I*, and wished to seek it out. Fantastic idea, I thought. Trip Withnail & I & Us was thus born, and I could hardly wait.

After organizing the food, tents, sleeping bags, and most importantly the music, we were off. We had a collection of tunes for all occasions: Morcheba, Café del Mar, The Levellers, Coldplay, and an assortment of ambient, trance, and house collections. Having just got on the main road Jim started to skin-up. I was a little apprehensive about this in case the police stopped us however I said nothing. After a few spliffs my anxiety gave way to apathy and then anticipation for the weekend ahead. The sun was shining, even though it was the middle of September, and with The Levellers playing loud I didn't have a care in the world. We joked, smoked, and sung the entire way there. Even

Vince, who was driving, accompanied Jim and I on drums with the help of the steering wheel.

By the time we needed help from the map it was already getting dark. We stopped a little way from what we thought was a power station to find our way. With the effects of the copious smokes we had consumed along the way and the lights from the power station strangely resembled the ship in *Close Encounters of Third Kind*, I thought. I used be quite an anorak in my time. I used to keep informed of the latest UFO news and sightings in magazines and videos. As such I shared this comparison with the others. "You would say that Jeff" Jim said with a smirk.

Having found our way, we drove down a little road by the edge of one of the lakes. Even in the dark the sight was truly spectacular. Vince pulled over so we could take in the view. The full moon was shining over the lake; it's reflection creating silver ripples.

"That's truly gorgeous. What a wonderful sight...I really hope we aren't the only ones being allowed to see this. Gaia, you are truly magnificent. Hay Vince, put on the Ambient collection – yeah, that's the one. 'Ettttuuuuuu...' Ah, spliff, just what I needed, ta Jim. Hhhhiiiiss...huaaahhh. 'Ettttuuuuuuuu...' What a perfect place!"

The combination of the view, the full moon, the loud ambient music, and spliffs was all just too much. We could no longer stay sat in the car. We all got out; leaving doors wide open, feeling with our bodies for the currents flowing from the music. Soon all three of us were moving to its pace and style: slow, spiritual, natural, and emotional. Incredibly stoned at this point, I happen to glance up at a collection of fir trees swaying slightly in the breeze. They, too, appeared to be moving to the rhythm of the currents. It was as if Gaia herself was playing with and teasing me at the same time. We danced together for well over half an hour. I said nothing to either Vince or Jim during this experience and nothing much about it after. This was meant for me only, and I was going to keep it as such.

After about another half-hour's drive we came to the metaphoric 'gates' of the Lake District. Even in the dark we could sense how touristy the site was. There were picnic tables and several tents already pitched up for the night. "We'll stay here tonight", Vince said as he turned the car into the packed car park. It was already late so we hurriedly put up our three-man tent almost completely in the dark, save for the car's headlights.

We awoke with the first light of the day to the sound of rushing water and kiddies playing. There's nothing quite like that first morning camping out in nature, awaking with a frozen nose and the fresh – almost frozen – air of the morn. After washing our faces in the stream we had camped almost on top of the night before we quickly packed up. We had no intention of being where anyone else was. As such we had quite a drive ahead of us as hikers and families were walking out in all directions.

Sensing Jim and my desire to make serious distance with people, Vince rummaged around for the map to plan our way. While I put breakfast together (cheese and tomato sandwiches) and made the tea, Jim rolled a valley-sized spliff. Full, warm, and subtly stoned, we made our way out of the 'valley of people'. Morcheba was playing loudly as we entered the valley with the island in the middle that featured in *Withnail & I*. Upon seeing this, our spirits lifted. We were on the right track and loved every minute of it. To celebrate this news Jim leaned back to me and said that he had a special surprise for us when we got nearer to the site that afternoon. I was too busy rolling up another spliff to wonder what it could be; yet I somehow knew I was going to like it whatever it was.

"Man this is the life! Chillin with my mates in Monty-land with phat tunes

a playin' and a big spliff a burnin'! ...Yes, I do, indeed, deem this to be accept-
able. Only acceptable Jeff? *smirk* Well, ok if you insist: I Love it! Where are
my sunnys? 'Jim pass my gigs 'ere would ya mate?' Yeah ...now I can enjoy the
view! That's better!

...This reminds me of my 21ˢᵗ up in the moors with Jo...yeah, with Jo...That's
the first time you thought of her for a while Jeff. Your point? Nothing just
sayin..."

We stopped off in a little village along the way for lunch. We needed
to get some vital supplies, although what I can't remember. I took this
opportunity to phone home and tell Mum of our progress. I had said
that I would check in when I got up there and I was going to keep my
word. After asking a local shop assistant, I found the only public pay
phone in the village. The call went well, I thought, and I made my way
back to the car.

As the light was beginning to fade we were almost there. We had
found the valley where Monty's 'country retreat' sat, however, we chose
to stay on the opposite side for now and investigate the next morning.
We drove down some more country lanes and passed some local youths
in a pick-up. Vince slowed down to chat to them in order to find out
specific directions. Although I had been smoking since before seven in
the morning and was subsequently completely high at this point, the
youths' chat went straight over my head. "It can't just be the weed", I
thought. After about five minutes Vince pulled his head back in and
drove on. "What canners man!" he said as he turned the music up again.
Apparently they had been smoking all morning too and were on the
lookout for some more weed. They couldn't have been more than seven-
teen, eighteen tops, but at least I felt reassured that I had not yet lost
the ability to comprehend speech. However, I was still with it enough
to grasp the irony of what Vince had said, even if no one else had
picked it up.

Before long we were driving up a dirt track, literally the end of the road and the end of the line as far as we were concerned. There was a shack or disused barn up ahead and we were going to make camp there. Rain clouds were rolling in and we had prepared a bar-b-que for that evening. We were going to need cover. After inspection we concluded it was an old abandoned barn once used for sheltering sheep, as white curly hair littered the ground.

Once unpacked, music and head lights left on in the car, Jim pulled out his surprise for us. There were two bags of tiny mushrooms curled up on his hands. Vince beamed a smile from ear to ear. "You star-man, nice one!" he exclaimed as he started brewing up a shroom-based tea. Jim handed Vince and I a handful and said "down these for starters", while passing us a bottle of beer. They tasted woody and gritty, yet I tried to ignore this and swigged them down. Magic mushrooms were the only other drug I was prepared to take, weed aside of course, after my 'induction' a few weeks before hand. Jim, like most philosophy students no doubt, was incredibly sensitive and showed a genuine interest in others. These were two good reasons why I really liked him and got on so well with him. I had talked about this with the others and he had obviously prepared this surprise mostly for my benefit. I was truly touched.

After taking them I gave Jim a hug and thanked him. As friends, as teachers, in the same circle, hugging and genuine signs of affection were not uncommon between us. Vince, Jim and I were completely straight; however this was normal for us.

As the chicken was beginning to sizzle and the shroom tea had been passed around, the rain started to come down in torrents. We huddled under the very leaky roof and tucked into our dinner. After dinner and the post-dinner spliffs had been consumed we ventured out into the rain for a surf. We didn't care; we had plenty of spare clothes and besides the thunder and lightning were far too tempting. During a change of tapes, Jim and I quickly put up our tent. I was wondering how long it would take for the shrooms to kick in as we knocked the tent pegs into what could only be described as granite and cleared away the plethora of stones. Thankfully it didn't last too long and neither did the rain.

Vince and Jim went into the car to skin-up. They turned the music up louder, and I stopped surfin'. I noticed that the sky seemed to have colours akin to an oil painting. Gaia was dancing about all around me and could feel a tingling in my senses. "Spidey was always my favourite", I thought as I took another drag on my Camberwell Carrot.

*"God this sky is so beautiful...God I'm so high...Jeff?...yeah? *chuckle* Look at the stars tonight. Look at the constellations! Man they are so full! You never get this in a city! ...S'up Orion?! ...S'up Little Bear?! I love us sitting out here looking up at the stars...man I wish my mind would just shut the fuck up for a minute so I can take it all in! Vince and Jim...they know the score...they just know it! Feel it! It's as if they're joining hands with thousands of others...looking up at the stars!*

...you feel it too Jeff! ...Look at them all!! What a rush! Jim, Vin-...My God!!! There are millions of us!!"

"Hay, don't you guys ever get the feeling that we aren't alone? I mean, feel like there are thousands of others doing just the same thing, right now, looking up at the same stars, knowing and feeling exactly the same thing!?"

"My God, he's cracked it already."

*"Yeah, mate we do, hop on man!... Hop on..." *smile**

"The circle is nothing compared to this! "My God, I never knew! I can't believe it! I can't believe it!!...why did no-one ever tell me?!..."

I stayed up in that state all night – dancing, surfing, and just feeling the entire world's population in this place – with me, with us, with Gaia and the Heavens.

"Yes man – now that's the perfect tune to sum it all up! Jeff, listen to the words...now that's spot on..."

8

On the Road Again

After making a quick visit to Monty's country retreat the following morning only to find that the rather bigoted and mindless old farmer that owned the land refused entry to anyone who sought it out, we returned home. I didn't care however – having stayed up all night and spliffs a going round as we drove I was in heaven with Gaia. The day was truly gorgeous and the clouds danced their own little dance – as if only for me.

Upon returning back I started to tell my new housemates about my global 'realization moment' in 'Monty land'. They were all thrilled and excited to hear about it and about how I chose to phrase it in particular.

A few days later and Vince had received some great news. A while ago he had entered a competition to drive a Ferrari F1 at Silverstone. Well, as it turned out – he won! He was thrilled and started making arrangements to stay at his parents' house overnight and go to Silverstone the next day as well as to skip a few lectures at uni. While I wasn't working still at the time and seeing as though he could bring one friend along for the ride, so-to- speak, he invited me along. I was really touched. He could have asked Jim, maybe he did already, but as it turned out either he couldn't go or suggested that I might like the experience. Either way I don't know but was eager to get on the road again.

We were on our way. As the effects of the spliffs started to kick in we chatted about everything and anything. The conversation then turned to Vince's history and background. As it turned out Vince had suffered from manic depression (or bi-polar as it is now called) in the past and had to be hospitalised. Whilst I had studied psychiatric conditions at uni – I knew very little about them in reality. "Poor bloke" I thought as we pulled into a service station for petrol and some snacks.

Whilst inside I found myself thinking about what Vince had told me about his past and also in the music section of the shop. "Get us some good tunes for the rest of our journey" I thought and give them to him – yea Jeff that might cheer him up. My attention soon focused on Bowie's greatest hits and I decided to purchase it. I had always loved Bowie's music ever since I could remember; it never failed to make a smile spread across my face. I'm sure I had heard Bowie's music in the womb as both my mother and Dad were big fans of his.

Once back in the car I showed Vince what I had bought for him. He was touched and stuck them on immediately. As we hit the road again the conversation turned to UFO's and psychic abilities. Vince, as it turned out, had visited a medium in London once and was telling me about the experience and about what she had told him. I then suggested that I would like to see her also and if we had the time we could make a detour there. He thought we might not have the time but said simply "we'll see" with a smile.

Soon it was getting dark and we were nearing Vince's parent's village where they lived. "Jeff before we get home I want to show you something" Vince then said rather cryptically. We pulled into a dark alley and parked the car at what appeared to be a row of hedges up ahead. Orion was in full view and my Spidey sense had begun to tingle immensely.

Leaving the car's headlights on and Bowie still playing Vince and I walked towards the hedge.

"Vince, what on Earth are you up to? Where are you taking me? I guess you'll find out soon Jeff. Look at the stars tonight – there is that oil painting again – Van Gogh is nothing compared to Gaia!"

Vince then led me to a section of the hedge through which we could pass through. On the other side was a steep grassy incline. "Follow me Jeff" Vince then said as he started to make his way to the top. After several minutes of stumbling up the incline we had made it to the top. "So, why have you taken me here Vince" I then asked. "Because of what you are standing on Jeff" he said.

Looking down at my feet I could just make out some broken cobble stones around them. "It's an old Roman road" Vince then said. "Roman road? Roman road my arse!" I said "it's a bloody UFO landing strip" I exclaimed as my gaze turned upwards into the Heavens. Vince chuckled but said nothing.

"Feel it Jeff, feel the energy around this place – it's electrifying. The ions in the air are dancing all about you – it's charging up for something big! Vince didn't bring you here to see an old road – it's something bigger – not of this world – he must know when and where it lands man!"

Vince sat on the edge of road in the grass and started to skin-up.

"See Jeff – he's not denying it! Listen to Bowie now – he's telling you – he knows what's going to happen...oh my God – look, look over there – at those lights – it's coming in – oh my God – Jeff get ready!"

In the sky, not too far away from us, were three coloured lights spaced out in a triangle: a red one, a blue one and a white one. They were slowly moving in unison from right to the left. I pointed them out to Vince who made several possible suggestions as to what they could be. "It's a helicopter" he finally concluded. I doubted that very much as it was too close and there was no sound of the rotor blades. We stared at it until it finally moved out of sight.

"Ok Jeff – we both know that it certainly wasn't a helicopter – but why didn't it land? Well Jeff – you were excited but also a tad scared shitless when you first saw it – maybe they picked up on that and decided that you weren't ready to see them yet – yea that's plausible man...you simply weren't ready Jeff!"

With that we slowly made our way back to the car. After getting back into the car we headed down some more country lanes until we got to gate and a bit of a driveway. We had made it to Vince's parent's house. One final spliff later we went inside to greet his parents. They were nice and polite and seemed happy to see Vince again. After eating a hearty meal, which they had prepared for us, we turned in early as we had a very busy day the next day.

9

Silverstone

For some reason I did not sleep very well that night. Either it was the excitement of the next day's proceedings or else there was something about Vince's parents' house that unnerved me. As I was walking up stairs the night before I noticed several pictures of old relatives adorned the walls on the stair case. It reminded me of Jo's big house where I had stayed at one Easter before our breakup. This, like that one, was truly a posh upper- class house I thought as I passed them.

When Vince and I both got ready we went down stairs and into the kitchen. Vince's father was already sitting at the table having his breakfast and his mother was standing by the stove. In the light of day I could now see what seemed like hundreds of postcards from all over the world adorned the walls by the breakfast table. Still feeling somewhat uneasy at this stage I tried to make some light conversation:

"Jeff – c'mon man – say something – the silence is killing me – yeah I know, but what? Why is his father staring at me like that? I dunno – but you gotta say something and fast!"

"That's quite an impressive collection of postcards you have there" I said to his father, "do you travel a lot then?" He told me that he used to for work and that Vince's older sister does too. General chit chat then followed which seemed to break the ice somewhat. During this time however, all I wanted to do was get out of there and start our day at Silverstone.

I soon got my wish. Before long we were saying our goodbyes and got in the car. As Vince was checking the map for directions I started to skin-up. "That house was far too like Jo's home for my liking" I thought as I lit the giant spliff I had just rolled. I then passed it to Vince as we started on our way.

It wasn't long before we were pulling into Silverstone's visitor's car park. It seemed like there were many other winners as the car park was almost full. We got out and made our way up to the visitors' centre. Once inside I made my way over to the table of teas and coffees and made myself a drink. After signing in we then all sat down and some guy started talking to us and welcoming us to Silverstone and told us about what we can expect for the day.

People then started going out for drives in the Ferrari F1. We had to wait our turn so we went outside and had a look around the place. It wasn't long before they called Vince's name on the loud speaker. With a big smile on his face Vince turned to me and said "I guess I'll see you later Jeff – you can watch me from up there if you like" as he pointed to some seats above the visitors' centre. I wasted no time in racing up there as I wanted to watch his lap in that magnificent machine. I then saw Vince come out of the bottom of the visitor's centre with a helmet on as he got into the passenger's seat.

As the Ferrari speed off into the distance at break neck speed I found it quite difficult to keep my eyes on it. The sound was deafening but I was well excited by this stage. When the Ferrari eventually did make it back to the start grid something quite amazing happened.

Vince got out of the passenger's side and into the driving seat! "Oh my God, he's going to drive that thing?!" I thought as Vince put metal to metal. In a blur they were off again – off into the distance. It was truly a magnificent sight to behold.

When Vince had returned back and found me up in the seats he was buzzing. I could just tell. "So – how was it?" I asked him. He gave me one of his enigmatic smiles and replied "you'll see" with a chuckle.

Before I had a chance to ask Vince any more questions about his experience I heard my name being called. "Oh my God this is it" I thought as I made my way into the visitor's centre to don my helmet. I walked down the stairs to the bottom of the centre and there facing me was the Ferrari F1; its engines humming. "Here goes nothing!" I thought as I climbed into the passenger's seat.

To say that we had 'taken off' was an understatement. When that accelerator hit the floor my head shot backwards into the headrest. "Fuck – this like taking off in an aeroplane" I thought. From corner to corner and from chicane to chicane I thought we were going to take off at any moment.

"Fuckin' hell Jeff – hold on tight – oh fuck stop smiling you stupid twat! Hehe I can't help it! Oh hello Spidey – are you going again? What now? What do you want? I've come to tell you Jeff that this is the life! Yea I know that – no you're not listening to me – this is the life that YOU need to lead! What? Become a racing car driver? No Jeff – you need to speed up your life – life is motion – life is speed – feel it inside you – feel it there in your heart now! The whole globe is spinning and now you feel it when you reach this speed – E=mc² man! Time travel – you can do it! Speed up your life man – speed up!"

Whew! Before I knew it we were back at the start line and the driver was talking to me. I had to do a double take about what he has asked me as it didn't sink in the first time around. "Say again" I asked as he repeated his offer for me to drive this beast.

"Oh my God Jeff – he's just given you the keys to the time machine! You know you can't drive man! Yea I know that – but this is no ordinary machine – it's the real thing man – H .G. Wells has nothing on me now man – Get a fuckin' grip – it's still a car and you don't even have a licence man! This is a big mistake – get a grip – ok ok Jeff and Spidey – calm the fuck down you both and let me think here..."

With that I turned to the driver and said that I would love to but I was too afraid of its power. His black visor just shone in my face as I heard him say that I was wise to be cautious.

I soon found Vince up on the same stand that I was on when I was watching his lap. "How come you didn't drive it mate" he then asked me. I was close to telling him my realization time travel moment whilst in the car and about how I was close to driving it – but I choose against it. I simply said "that beast was too powerful for me man" and left it at that.

After visiting the shop there at Silverstone for a few souvenirs we headed for home. The usual spliffs and chatter then ensued and we had made good headway before Vince pulled over and said that he needed some sleep. I was a little put off by this as we were so close to being home but I let it go. I got out of the car and sat on the bank, joint in hand. My mind then wondered back to Vince's house in the country.

Vince, however, soon woke up – much to my surprise and we were on our way again. Before long we had reached back home and we went inside.

10

The Drug 'Cult-ure'

Once inside we recounted our story and journey to Silverstone to the rest of our housemates. Jim, in particular, found it very interesting when I told him about my theory of the speed of life and how I came by it. My other two housemates, Jack (a red-headed guy studying engineering) and Heather (another dreadlock housemate who was taking Art) both seemed to revel in the story about the UFO above the Roman road.

After eating our evening meal we all then went upstairs for fresh filter coffee and post dinner spliffs. At this point not only was my attention focused on Café del Mar playing softly in the background but also on how Heather was rolling the joint.

"The art of rolling is indeed an art form – you got that right Jeff – look at how Heather is rolling hers compared to how you do it – I bet she could enter a movie of herself rolling one and submit it as her final year project and get great marks for it – you really think so Jeff? Yea why not? Well because the establishment usually frowns upon drugs and the old ways and art forms man – that's why..."

I shared my observation with everyone and a conversation started about the establishment, the system in general and then about the monarchy. My mind then wondered back to what my Mum had said about my grandmother sending her our family tree. As it turned out there has always been some story in the family about way back when, on their side of the family, there was some relative who used to work at a royal house and then suddenly left with enough money to buy a house and bore a child. This relative, as it turned out, was only a maid or servant so how she could afford such a house was beyond any of our comprehension. Could we be related to the royal family in some way? We sometimes thought.

I then began to feel uneasy about the way the conversation was going. All the people in the room apart from me, it seemed, were not exactly in favour of the existence of the monarchy.

I then made some excuse and went downstairs. As I sat on my bed my mind was racing with thoughts:

"I'm so sorry your Royal Highness...we may be related and I can't listen to this talk. This is insulting to you and Grandma and to our whole lineage maybe. Fuck I need some air – go to the park Jeff – ok man let's go..."

I got up slowly making sure I could still hear the others upstairs talking. They were. I made my way down to the front door only to find that it was locked and bolted. "Fuck – I need to get out and now!" I thought as I searched for the key. After what seemed like ages I found it and unlocked the door.

As soon as I stepped out; "bang!"

"Fuck me! What was that? A gunshot Jeff, someone is shooting at you! Who the fuck could be shooting at you? Someone doesn't want you to leave – but why? Because of your royal connection Jeff – it has to be – it's a fuckin'

conspiracy to get to you! Grandma must have been right – the whole thing man – wake up!! This house is a cult! A drug-cult! That's what the fucking circle is all about...oh my God...and who is the head of it? Steve! It must be him shooting at you – he doesn't live far - it could easily be him Jeff! Man you need to get out of here and fast! Fucking hell Jeff what the fuck have you gotten yourself into?..."

My heart was racing to a point where I thought it would burst out of my chest. Beads of sweat started dripping down my forehead as I scrambled back inside and up to my room.

"Find your fucking mobile Jeff – call your Bro – ask him to get you and fast – you need to get the fuck out of here and now!"

After trying to remain a bit calm and telling my Bro that I wanted to come home he said he would pick me up and as soon as he can. I packed my things as fast as I could and paced back and forth by the front door with it just ajar. There was no way I was going outside for Steve to take another shot at me but I needed to see when my Bro's car would turn up.

It wasn't long before I saw his car. I dropped the keys on the kitchen table and ran towards it. Once inside I thanked him profusely. It was already dark by this point and I was sure that the others back at the house were on our tail. "Please Bro – go faster" I thought as I turned round to see if I recognised Vince's or Steve's car behind us. "We must have lost them" I thought as we pulled over to park by my Mum's house. We were home and I felt a bit safer.

II

Back Home

When I got in I went immediately to the couch we had in our dining room and sat down. I then began to rock back and forth uncontrollably as my Mum asked my Bro what had happened. She then turned her attention to me and asked me the same thing. The best I could do at that point was to say that I got scared and left it at that. I then believe she made a few phone calls trying to get some kind of help but the outcome of which would only become apparent the next morning. I couldn't listen or take in anything much that night as my mind was racing – as was my heart and breathing.

Before too long she then suggested I try and get some rest. I made my way slowly to the bedroom upstairs. The full length dressing mirror in the room for some reason scared me and so I asked for something to cover it. Mum found a Chinese throw that I blue- tacked to the mirror. That seemed to do the trick and I got into bed. "Try and get a good night's sleep" she said as she closed the door behind her. My mind was racing with the day's events as I stared out of the window. That also seemed to scare me a bit so I closed the curtains almost fully closed but save for some moonlight coming into the room and falling on my bed.

"That's better Jeff, for all you know they could be out there if they did manage to follow you – but you need some light in here."

For about what seemed like hours I tossed and turned in bed replaying the day's events. At some point I did manage to fall asleep however but I did not sleep well at all; not good quality sleep at any rate.

After what only seemed like an hour or two sleeping I heard someone knocking at my door. It was light and I heard Mum's voice saying "Are you awake yet?" I replied that I was. I got dressed slowly and then made my way downstairs.

After a cup of tea and a few cigs later I found out what had happened with the phone calls my Mum had made the night before. As it turned out, Mum had made an emergency G.P. appointment for me this morning. She had rearranged a meeting she had at work to go with me. We were leaving in about an hour.

My Bro then got up and came downstairs and started to make his breakfast quickly. He was late for work and so we didn't chat much about last night's events. To be honest, I was glad of that.

Before long my Bro had gone to work and my Mum and I were on our way to the doctor's. My leg was jiggling up and down as I looked around and behind us. "What are you looking for?" Mum then asked me. "Nothing" I replied as I didn't want to worry her.

"Man I hate going to the doctor's. The building looks like a mortuary and the patients all look about ready to be visiting it soon. And that doctor, Dr Foster, looks like Peter Cushing in one of his horror films."

"Man he's scary. I can't go in there – that's it – I'm not going. Well what are you going to say to Mum? Jeff, just say that you feel better now – yea that might work..."

After a few minutes pleading with Mum to take me back home I realised that I was fighting a losing battle with her. Regrettably, we were soon called in the doctor's room and I was dreading every minute of it. There he was, sat upright in his chair with his piercing eyes and his Peter Cushing face and hair. My leg started to jiggle again as Mum started to recount the events of the night before.

After he had asked me a few questions about the events of the night before and about how I was feeling now he then asked to speak to Mum alone. Perhaps I had blagged my way out of it after all I thought as I went outside for a cig.

It wasn't long before Mum joined me and we were on our way home again. Mum was a little upset with me I could sense as she asked me why I did not go into any details of the night before or about how I was feeling now. Either she was upset, disappointed or simply didn't believe what I had told the doctor. She then proceeded to tell me that an appointment had been made for me to see a junior psychiatrist in the next few days. "Fine" I thought as we pulled into our driveway. I could blag them just as easily as I did with Peter Cushing in there. Besides – I don't need any fucking psychiatrist – I just need to get away from the drug cult I had unwittingly fallen into.

Over the next few days I spent my time staying busy with things. Mum had prepared me a list of things to do each day which ranged from cleaning, cooking to gardening. When I had finished my daily list I often spent the evenings going for walks in my local neighbourhood and up to the field and woods near the house. I felt safe then that Steve and Co. had not found where I lived now so I could do this with relative ease. That said I often found myself thinking about how very lonely I was now and how no one truly understood me. I couldn't tell my Mum and Bro about the circle and about the cult that Steve and Co. had gotten me into for their sake. The less they know the safer they are I thought. Besides, it would only worry them further and that was the last thing I wanted to do.

12

The School of Life

The day soon came when I was due to see the junior psychiatrist, Dr. Smith. This time my Mum had given me some change to get a taxi there as she had to be in work that day. I didn't mind too much about that except the fact that where the taxi took me was close to where Steve and Co. lived. My anxieties started to rise.

Once inside however my anxiety levels lowered. Dr. Smith, as it turned out, was an odd sort. For starters I was convinced that she had some kind of lazy eye or else she had the propensity to cross her eyes at times. She also appeared to have some kind of tick – by that I mean her head moved in a somewhat erratic fashion at times. While I spent most of the time blagging my way through the answers I gave her I couldn't help thinking that she was crazier than I was.

When I had returned home it was only 11am and I started on my list of things to do for that day. Before long I heard the post come through the letterbox at the front door so I went to collect the mail. I found that there was a letter for me stamped from the university. I read it there and then. As it turned out the university was offering me the opportunity to do re-takes for my final year exams. I was in two minds as to whether or not to throw it straight into the bin but choose against it.

"*Jeff, I know you said you would never do exams again but you are feeling slightly better these days man. You could study for a bit and then go take one – today even. It is exam time now I'm sure of it – get one out of the way. Yea you think so? Yea I'm sure of it – why not study for your abnormal psychology module now...you can do it.*"

With that I wasted no time in getting out my text books and notes and sat down at the dining room table. "Ok – here goes" I thought as I started to read the competing theories about the aetiology and psychopharmacology of schizophrenia and depression.

"*Yea Jeff – you know the score – you have always been good at knowing about these two conditions in particular. One of them is bound to turn up in the exam so just learn about these two in depth. Yea – man – that's a good idea Jeff...*"

As it was nearing lunchtime I was still heavily into my revising:

"*Ok, the 6 main categories are: genetic, prenatal, social, drug abuse, psychological and neural. Neural is still the most widely held theory today (albeit not exclusively) as it offers opportunities to correct the imbalance of neurotransmitters in the brain. This has been spurred on by the Dopamine Hypothesis of Schizophrenia which states that a possible increase in activation of the D_2 receptors can cause the positive symptoms of schizophrenia. Dopamine eh? Didn't Grandpa have to take L-Dopa for his Parkinson's disease – yea I think he did Jeff...Perhaps Schizophrenia and Parkinson's are related in some way Jeff...they very well could be...*"

At which point I started to feel my mind wandering off and thinking about my Grandpa on my mother's side. He was diagnosed with Parkinson's disease when I was very young and so I only could remember him with the disease. When I was about 6 or 7 he was suffering badly from it by then and was in a wheelchair sitting in his bedroom most of the day. At that age I didn't understand the condition at all and his inability to talk much and his hand shaking sometimes scared me. Still, he was my Grandpa and I loved him very much. I remembered all the chess games we used to play in his room when I sometimes used to cheat. I then felt a wave of sadness sweep over me as I stopped studying and went upstairs to the toilet.

"I'm so sorry Grandpa for the times I took advantage of your condition and cheated at chess with you. It wasn't until talking to Mum some years later after you passed away then I began to realise that you were very much still with it only that your body was falling apart around you. How horrible and frustrating that must have been for you Grandpa. If I can find a cure for Parkinson's maybe that will go some way towards making amends with you...I miss you Grandpa...what was that song you used to play for me? About the fastest milkman in the west?"

I had remembered the song as I started to make my way downstairs and into the kitchen. "I want to do this for you Grandpa" I thought as I picked up my notes I had been writing and revising with and started on my way to uni. "I know I know all my stuff" I thought as I started to walk from Mum's house to uni. Every so often I would glance at my notes just to make sure but somehow I always got the answer right that I had asked myself. "See Jeff – it's all there – just trust in the process as Mum always tells you – you will do fine".

After about half an hour I was nearing uni. The sun was shining down and I felt warm and safe and that somehow Grandpa was with me. As I made my way to the exam hall I suddenly felt as if I knew what was going to happen:

"Grandpa – I know you are helping me now and I know that you will help me to do well on the exams...but how? Wait Jeff – it's obvious – he is going to

be there! In the hall with you – don't worry though – it will only be just you and him. He will be your invigilator – just you and him. Relax Jeff – relax your beating heart man – everything is going to be fine."

As I got to the doors of the exam hall I remembered that Grandpa was a teacher and that even where he was now he was still teaching me – helping me – in my studies. "Yes – just you and him Jeff" I thought as I opened the door and went inside.

It was deathly quiet. I then started to make my way up the stairs to the main exam room. Feeling very edgy and nervous about meeting Grandpa again I somehow knew that he was going to be okay now – free from his Parkinson's – standing at the front of the hall in front of my desk. I took a deep breath and opened the door.

Nothing. There were no desks and most importantly no Grandpa.

"What are you missing Jeff? I still feel you Grandpa – so what have I missed? Have I misunderstood you? Or is it something else? Psychology Jeff – think man think! It must be something to do with the school of psychology...go there man – c'mon Jeff – work it out – what are you missing?"

I slowly made my way back down the stairs and out towards the school of psychology.
As I was passing the sign to the school I stopped and stared at it.

"Bla Bla University, School of Psychology – school, school of psychology...what is it trying to me – what are you trying to tell me Grandpa? Well, what have you been doing at uni? I mean why do people go to uni Jeff? Let's work it out from the start man...well to learn – to learn about what they want to do in life...yea, and, so? So they are learning about life – that's what uni is for – and the school Jeff? Bingo man! That's the discipline through which they learn this lesson! You Jeff have been learning about life through psychology – you have been learning about your own life through going through

psychological processes – through psychological states – through psychological conditions Jeff! No wonder everyone thinks you're mad!"

"Think about it...ok, but what am I missing? It's simple Jeff – you haven't finished – you haven't officially finished your lesson. But I got my degree man – yes you got your degree but you still want to do more exams even after you said you were finished with them! Everyone gets an ordinary degree – the trick is to realise this and move on with your life – just stop studying Jeff! Just be free man and live! For fuck sake! Ok, but what am I missing...?"

My attention focused back onto the doors of the psychology building and then onto the main reception desk. "Jeff your library card! Man – you haven't given it back yet! Fuck Jeff – you've got it! Give your card back man!" With that I shot straight into the building and gave my card back. I then walked out and headed for home with a big sigh of relief and a big smile on my face. I had finished my studies – my life's lesson – and I was beaming along with the sunshine. Thank-you Grandpa!

13

The Ninja Bet

When I had returned home I sat by the dining room table and lit a cig. My attention soon wandered back to the re-takes form lying in front of me and something caught my attention. It was the price. To do the re-sits it would cost me £125 quid. I hadn't paid it and knew that I only had exactly £120 quid in my account. I was £5 quid short. "That's why I couldn't do my exams" I thought even though I didn't want or need to now.

"A fiver eh Jeff – that's all that's been stopping you from taking your re-sits? What's the significance of the fiver? Think Jeff – it must be something you've done man – think about it...oh my God – do you remember the Ninja bet you made way back when you were into Ninjas? You bet your Bro a fiver that you would become a Ninja by the time you were 21! And that's in a few weeks time man! Yea Jeff – but I was only about 9 or 10 when I made that bet. Yea Jeff maybe so – but that fiver has been stopping you all this time...It's fucked up your studies man because unconsciously you have been trying to fulfil this stupid bet! Psychologically crippling you and diverting yourself from your true path in life!"

"Man Jeff – it's so obvious now – and that's why you lost Jo! You were

meant to be with her – and if it wasn't for that fucking bet you would be now man! You were destined to be with her Jeff and you've fucked it all up! You need to cancel this bet and fast!"

With that I grabbed my cigs and headed out again. I had a long walk in front of me to get into town and cancel the bet with my Bro (who was working there). "It just has to be done" I thought as I quickened my pace.

As the light started to fade the cars along the road by which I was walking turned on their lights. I remember thinking that I needed help from somewhere or someone as an unknown force seemed to be pushing me away from town. "Steve and Co. are not going to stop me from this" I thought. I then suddenly felt that people were staring at me from all the cars passing me by. Instead I choose to focus on their headlights and back lights.

"Jeff man – pay attention only to the cars' lights and to other lights around you for help man. Yea – there's a blue light – you know who that represents don't you? Who Jeff – Jo! Of course – her favourite colour, and green – the healing colour for Grandpa, red – passion – for your Bro and white – the divine light for your Mum. They all are helping you get into town now man. Don't let them down!"

Then, as I was half way there, I heard I had received a text on my mobie. It was from Vince! "Fuck Jeff they are onto you man! Walk faster...fuck that run Jeff run!!" My heart was racing and my breathing joined suit as I ran and ran – across roads and intersections – I didn't care – I just had to get to my Bro and like yesterday.

As I got into the outskirts of town I must have ran for about 20 minutes solid. I was exhausted and very thirsty. Up ahead I could see another set of traffic lights – they were on red – but this time I stopped. I couldn't run anymore. As I pushed the button for the lights to change

I noticed that there – sitting on the traffic light box – was a glass of water. "Thank you!" I said as I downed the water and kept on going.

When I got to the shop where my Bro was working I went straight inside and found him. I must have looked quite a sight as my Bro was shocked to see me. After saying that I needed to speak with him urgently we both left the shop and sat on a bench outside. My hand was shaking as I tried to roll a cig. "Here have one of mine!" my Bro then said as I started to remind him about the ninja bet. "What the fuck is this is all about?" he then said as he said to me. He couldn't even remember me making the bet with him. Not wanting to scare him I pulled out a fiver I had gotten from the cash machine when I got into town. "You win" I said as I gave him the £5 quid note. "Man, go home, I will be finishing work soon and we can talk about this there" he then said.

With that – I got up and started to walk home. I had done it – the bet was off and I could relax albeit with one eye over my shoulder in case Steve and Co. were following me. After about 45 minutes I was safe at home as I heard the keys turn in the front door. It was Mum.

14

⟨⟨⟩⟩

Night of the Long Knives

After my Bro had gotten back home from work he proceeded to tell my Mum what had happened earlier that evening. I think I thought I had done a pretty good job blagging about it and saying that I fancied a walk into town and then remembered about the ninja bet so gave him the fiver. That was enough – we then ate dinner and I decided to take an early night. I was exhausted from the day's activities.

The next day my mind was still racing over the events of the day before. "Had I saved my life yesterday?" I thought and "would I get Jo back?" Just before my Mum went to work the phone rang. It was her sister, my aunty, the farmer. After talking with her for a bit my Mum then asked if I would like a chat with her. I wasn't too sure if I did or not as my mind was racing but I did anyway. My Mum had sought her advice, it transpired; about what to do with me the night before and now my aunty was suggesting that I started to think about getting benefits because I wasn't working and about taking some kind of medication. I think I said that I would think about it and left it at that.

Before long I was alone in the house again and with my 'to do' list. I did a few of the 'chores' as they had become on the list and sat down around lunchtime. I then pushed the list aside and lit a cig. Something was not right. I should feel happier than I did at this point. I had finally gotten rid of uni from my life and had successfully finished my life's lesson in psychology. I also had paid my bet off with my Bro – so both of these factors couldn't be the reason for my feelings I thought. Then it dawned on me:

"Yes Jeff, you have got rid of those two elements from your life but you are missing or forgetting something...your past here – in this city! It must be that – you will have to undo all the mistakes you have done whilst you were in a fucked up state spurred on by the bet man!"

With that I went straight upstairs and into my bedroom.

"Ok what is wrong in here? That bloody hat! My poetry hat! Steve gave that to you man – it must be cursed – get rid of that for starters. Ok now what else...nothing that I can think of Jeff. Yea what about where you lived before – what you mean the house we rented before Mum bought this one you mean? Yea – you will have to go there and undo the mistakes you have done there!"

I went downstairs grabbed my cigs and headed out for the rented house. I thought about the conversation I had with my aunty and about what I needed to do in order to undo all the mistakes in this city. It was going to be a long day but didn't care. It had to be done if my life was ever going to be ok again.

About half way to the rented house I started to feel a sharp pain in my foot. Panic started to set in as I thought that someone was trying to harm me or stop me from achieving my goals that day.

"Fuck Jeff – what the fuck is that? It feels like a burning knife is pricking the sole of your foot – are you sure its just your foot it's hurting – well no I'm not – it's burning my very soul too I feel – who the fuck could be doing this? It's some kind of voodoo for sure – could it be Steve and Co.? I don't think

so Jeff – they don't know what you are trying to do today man. Ok – who else could it be then? Well who have you spoken to today? Mum, my Bro and my aunty. There ya go man – your aunty – it could be her – but why? 'Cuz you know you are a worry to your family now and you put her Mum – your Grandma in jeopardy with the whole circle/cult thing! Oh fuck – and she's a farmer – she knows nature – she knows nature voodoo – you have to go to the benefits office man – you have to! But what about the rented

house – well you'll just have to do that another time man – do what she said first...Owww this really hurts..."

With that thought I turned as if being ridden like a horse with a bit a in my mouth. My tongue then went over my teeth and I felt a dip in my teeth about half the way back on my right side. It wasn't a hole or anything like that – but rather where a bit had grinded down my teeth in that place over time. "Ok aunty, I'm going – I'm fucking going!" I thought as the pain from my foot started to make it difficult for me to walk.

After a backbreaking and agonising 20 minutes I passed the area in the north of the city where *The Pilgrimage* had occurred all those weeks back now. I'm not going anywhere near that venue I thought – I'm not letting Steve and Co. catch me now. I've come so far. But while I'm here I could stop off at my local dealer's house and make amends with him. I walked – or rather hobbled by then up to his front door and rang the bell. I thought I owed him some money so I was going to square it with him. After ringing the bell again, the door opened and the sounds of Jimi Hendrix wafted out – as did copious amounts of dope smoke.

I explained why I was there but he said I was all square with him. I felt confused. He then offered for me to come inside but I thought against it as another sharp jab of the knife in my shoe made me wince. "Ok aunty – I'm going now I'm fucking going".

Another 20 minutes or so and I was in town. By now my foot was numb with pain as I started to think about what I needed to do in town. "Your first job in town was with that insurance company. Yea ok Jeff lets go there and talk with my ex-colleagues." I went to the building and into the front lobby. There to my surprise was a band of elderly gentlemen all wearing poppies to remember the fallen in the world wars. "What does this mean?" I thought as I stood there not knowing quite what to do. I then fumbled around for a few change in my wallet and dropped it into one of the buckets they held. "Thank-you son" came the reply. I knew that Grandpa had been in Germany during the Second World War and so I gained a bit of comfort from that, and that I had done enough here.

It didn't last long however. The next place I had to go to was the internet entertainment company and apologise to the boss and my ex-colleagues there. Perhaps I could ask for my job back, I thought. As I went up in the lift I thought about that's where I still would be if it weren't for that stupid bet and me falling into the drug cult. Jo would want me to still be here I thought as I walked out onto our, well, my old office level.

It then suddenly dawned on me that I didn't have swipe card any longer as I had handed it in when I left there. Exhausted I went into the toilets and washed my face with water. The pain in my foot had returned also and I fell to my knees, almost sobbing.

"Oh aunty, what the fuck do you want from me? I have tried to undo all the things I have done wrong – and I want this job back so that Jo could be proud of me. Not just her but also her Mum – I know they both come from a very wealthy family."

With that – I suddenly realised that Jo's Mum had horses and it became increasingly likely that it wasn't my aunty that was doing the voodoo at all but rather Jo's Mum all the time! But why...?

"Because of how you have treated her daughter Jeff – wake up and smell the coffee man! You were there when you both drank to excess and smoked weed all the time. You even bought it for her. Yea once, as a present Jeff! Yea well ok – but still – you corrupted her man – no wonder she went onto coke just before you two split up. You are too powerful an influence on her – what with your royal connections man! It's so obvious now – it's her Mum doing this to you!"

Remorse and regret then swept over me like a torrent – a tidal wave – a flood. "Purge yourself Jeff – do it for Jo's sake – show her Mum how sorry you are! – but how? Well..." I looked up and found myself staring at the toilet bowl. "If you really loved Jo then you would be puking at the thought of what you have done – so go on – puke – puke you bastard!!!" With that I started putting fingers down the back of my throat and tried to make myself puke. All I got was the dry heaves (as I had not eaten anything that day.) I sat there sobbing on the toilet floor.

"No way Jeff – you'll have to do better than that – finish your quest – you still have Brian to find". Brian was a family friend who lived on a houseboat and sometimes came to visit us. I had once smoked weed with him whilst working on his boat one day and felt I had to make amends. With that I slowly got up and left the building.

It was now dark outside and I made my way over to the canal. I knew that Brian sometimes used to moor his boat in a particular spot but in the darkness I couldn't find the place. I suddenly came across another boat called 'Oasis' painted in blues and whites.

"That boat is painted in the colours of the police. Perhaps Jo's Mum has sent it here for you Jeff. She now knows all about what you have done to her daughter and now she is out for revenge. But why a boat? Why not a car? Well Jeff – you are not going to the police station, but rather you are going to Manchester where Steve used to get his drugs from. You have to severe that

connection. Then back here? No man – then onto London...you have commit-ted treason in Jo's Mum's eyes and in the Queen's eyes too Jeff! You are going to be beheaded. Come on Jeff, get on the boat, we haven't got all night..."

With that I stepped onto the boat and tried to go inside. When I realised that the door was locked I heard someone shouting at me. I looked up and over at the next boat about a hundred yards away. There was a woman shouting at me to get off the boat; "Perhaps she is a friend of Brian's man – she is helping you..." I quickly got off the boat and walked briskly away from it.

When I was a safe distance away I sat down by the canal under a street-light. I always felt a bit safer in the light.

"Jeff man – you still have to go to London to face the music – why don't you swim there – what you mean? In the canal? Why not Jeff? Well for starters it will be cold and I doubt I could swim the entire way there. And besides, I need a slash."

I got up and went under a bridge to relieve myself. I felt a bit better. My mind then started to think about how I could get out of going to London. "I need help from somewhere" I thought as I started heading back into town. I felt exhausted by then and my foot was throbbing in pain. I just suffered through it however. My mind then wondered to some internet conversation I had had with a psychic online a day or two ago who said I would find help near a market or place with stalls. "The market!" I thought – "you have to make it there Jeff" as I turned in that direction.

Thankfully it wasn't long before I turned into the outdoor market. I then saw two figures sitting on a bench. They were the only people in the market as all the stalls had closed several hours ago now. I headed in their direction. "I can't go on anymore" I thought as I neared the couple. As it transpired they were two homeless people – a man and woman both drinking strong cider out of a cheap plastic bottle. I then started sobbing uncontrollably as they beckoned me over to sit with them.

I started to tell them about the night's events. I didn't care at this point if Jo's Mum or the Queen knew about this. I was exhausted and emotionally drained. I just couldn't take any more. "It will be all ok laddy" the man then said to me with a smile. The woman then put her arms around me and handed me the bottle they were both drinking from. I hadn't drunk anything in days but thought I could definitely use a drink now. "There ya go" she said sweetly as the man started to tell me a joke. He reminded me of Billy Connolly in his mannerisms and how he swore a lot but I felt safe with them.

After about half an hour talking and laughing with my new friends they said they had to go to the shop for some more cider. I felt bad that I had drunk some of their night's supply so I offered to give them some money towards their next purchase. "Save your money laddy" the man said "and keep the drink – you look like you need it more than we do right now" he said as they shuffled out into the darkness with a wave.

I sat there finishing off the cider and my cig. At that point I looked down at my feet and saw that my right shoe was covered in blood on one side. Ouch – the pain of the knife in my sole then came back to me. I then took off that shoe and removed my sock to look at the damage. I heard something make a noise on the ground near me as I looked at my blood stained foot. Whatever that was I thought it had made a big hole in both my sock and the bottom of my foot. After pouring the last of the cider on the wound I put my sock and shoe back on. It felt a bit better. "Ok Jeff – you need to go home – your Bro and Mum will be getting worried by now. What about London and Jo's Mum? Well – if they want to come and get you they can – but I just can't do anything more today."

With that I got up and started to make my way home. After about another 45 minutes later I had returned home. The Night of the Long Knives, it seemed, was over.

15

Upper Class Etiquette

When I got in Mum was sitting at the dining room table with my brother. They then asked me where I had been and I could sense that they were both very worried by this point. I didn't know what to say for the best. I certainly couldn't tell them what had really happened for their sake I thought. So kept quiet and said nothing. Dinner had been saved for me so I ate it on my own in the dining room. I thought this way I could avoid any further questions. After dinner I made my way up to bed – I needed rest and fell asleep without much difficulty that night.

The next day was Saturday. Mum had organized to go round to our neighbour's house all day. As it turned out their daughter was getting engaged tomorrow and wanted Mum to be there for the preparations today. They were a Hindu family and in their tradition these types of events took days to prepare.

When I got up Mum was already round there and my Bro was no-where in sight. There – on the dining room table was another list of things to do together with a note. It was from Mum pleading with me not to leave the house today and that she was right next door if I needed anything. I put the radio on (BBC Radio 2 of course) and started listening to the Toggmeister himself Mr Terry Wogan and started staring out through the patio doors into the garden.

"Gaia I love you – I really do. You still love me don't you? So did I save my life from Jo's Mum now? And the Queen? Well – they haven't come after you Jeff – that's true...where's that music coming from now?"

"Next door Jeff – it has to be – well I certainly hear all the traffic coming and going there...yep – they must be having lots of visitors round. You got that right man."

I then found myself thinking about nature, Gaia and love. My thoughts then turned to Jo as I started to doodle a diagram on the note my Mum had left me. I had a theory. I had been looking after our garden now for about week or so and it was in good shape. The back garden – the way I was facing – was the future and the front garden – behind me – was the past. Nature and Gaia represented love and nature the part of love which needs cultivating in order to grow. Whilst I had made good progress in the garden facing me I had neglected the garden behind me – the past – my past loves I surmised. Just look at the Queen's gardens Jeff – they are all immaculate – you need to emulate that and things in your life and love life will then be better – just like how next door's garden is immaculate.

I then remembered how my Mum's last partner was a gypsy from abroad. She had met him when we were living there in my teens. He was in touch with nature I thought and so is your aunty! And let's not forget your Grandma who studied biology at Cambridge! Our family are all very good with nature and you must learn this lesson now Jeff I thought as I started to make my way to the front garden to mow the lawn and pull some weeds out. I could feel my Grandpa close by and the gypsy helping me perhaps psychically in some way – both urging me onwards.

After about two hours of gardening I went in doors to have lunch. I was starving. I had skipped breakfast and so was ready for the lunch Mum had fixed for me earlier that morning. The radio was still on and I suddenly got the impression that it too was urging me on. Not to do gardening this time but rather like to smarten up my manners like the royals do. I placed out the silverware on the table in the correct fashion and sat down to eat. "If I do this Jeff – then maybe, just maybe, Jo would want you back" I thought.

It then dawned on me that food too was a source of love as it sustains us all. Moreover, it had been a part of my existence back at the drug cult house that I had neglected big time. "No wonder Jo hasn't come back to you Jeff – you have been starving yourself of love man" I thought as I finished what was on my plate and then wiped my mouth before taking a drink of the orange juice in front of me.

"Call her Jeff! Should I? Yes why not? Well she hasn't texted or called me since that text ending things with me...So what? That's because you have neglected yourself, your job, your health and love itself. But you are making amends now and you even have your family and the royal family on your side now – they all want you to succeed! Ok man – where's my mobie...?"

I went over to the counter and picked up my mobie. I had a text so I pressed the button to get to the text message section. It was from Vince again! Panic started to set in as I then heard fireworks go off at our neighbours next door! "What the fuck are they celebrating for? Are they in league with Vince and Steve and Co.?" I thought as I felt like I needed to get out of there. I dropped my mobie on the floor, grabbed my cigs, and left the house. "Where can you go Jeff? Well you need some more cigs – you can go to the local shop and get some more. Yea that's a good plan..." I thought as I started to walk faster to the shop.

Once inside the shop I bought the rolling tobacco and was just about to leave when I heard another big firework go off. I turned round to the shop keeper and looked at his red dot in the middle of his forehead as he smiled at me.

"Shit Jeff – they are all in league with them! It's not her fiancé that she wants – it's you man! Steve and Co. must have told her about your royal connections man! No fucking way – I want Jo – not her! I know but you have to go back home – Mum might be back soon and you have to start making dinner!"

By now I was shit scared that Steve and Co. were nearby and that they had somehow managed to convince next door's daughter to want to marry me. "That way they will have me just where they want me!" I thought as I raced home.

I had to stay occupied and clear my thoughts of next door. That's how she was urging me on to come to her and get engaged with her – through telepathy – I thought as I started making dinner. "They aren't going to win Jeff, be strong" I thought as I went into our garden for comfort and to be closer to Gaia, to our family, and to Jo. As I started to bend down and pick some chives for that night's meal I had a fleeting thought of revenge and payback. "Come and fucking get me if you want to Steve but leave my family and Jo out of this – this is between you and me!"

I went inside and started to chop the chives with our sharpest knife. All of sudden I looked down and saw blood mixed in with the green stalks. "Fuck ok Steve – is that the best you can do?!!" While I was putting on a brave face – I was secretly scared shitless by now of Steve's power and that feeling remained for several hours.

16

The Masonic Way

Soon I heard Mum's keys in the door and she stepped into the kitchen. I immediately noticed that her hands were done up in henna tattoos and she had on her sari dress. "You look nice" I said as I took another drag on my cig. "Thank-you - dinner smells nice" she said as she went upstairs – to change no doubt.

About a half an hour later my Bro then came through the door. He had been out with friends for the day. When dinner was ready we each got a tray and went to eat in the lounge. This was the norm round at ours as the dining room was mainly used for special occasions and when we had guests over. My Bro then put the telly on as we sat down to tuck in. Who wants to be a millionaire was on with Chris Tarrant and his cheesy grin spread across his face as usual.

"I hate this show...in fact I hate watching TV full stop. I wish he would stop looking at me...Jeff – was that a wink? I dunno man – but I'm looking away – yea good idea man...Mum why are you looking at me too? I can see you out of the corner of my eye...what is it? What do you want? I bet I'm making her feel uneasy 'cuz I'm not watching the show...well ok – I'll watch for a bit then – if I have to!"

As I started to watch the TV again I could see more often than not that Chris was winking at me – urging me on to answer the questions. "But why?" I thought as I could sense Mum looking at me again out of the corner of my eye.

"They want you to play the game Jeff! Ok I will but why all the winking? What is he trying to tell me? This is too unreal for my liking...it's like he can see me here sitting in our lounge – he's trying to get my attention!"

With that thought Chris' face started to morph into my Dad's face! I can't describe to you how it felt but for a few seconds it really happened. "Dad – it's you!" I thought "Ok I will try my best to play – but why Dad? Why do you want me to play? 'Cuz you will win for the family if you do Jeff! You will then be able to get Jo back man too – you will then be in her league!" I thought as I started to concentrate on the questions and answers.

Before long I was up to £64,000. I was getting really excited by this point but I tried not to show it. Dad didn't want me to let on that I knew it was him or else the whole show would be off. The whole deal would be off. I therefore kept a dead-pan poker face as I sat there watching and trying to answer then next question. Mum shot me another glance – I felt the pressure really being on now.

Then – disaster – I got the question wrong! That was it – the deal was off. I got up and left the room and sat down at the dining room table. I felt gutted – completely and utterly gutted. I lit a cig and almost came to tears. I then heard my Mum asking where I was and saying that there is a comedy show coming on next as she made herself a coffee. "I will be there in a bit" I said. Bless her; she's trying to console me I thought as I rolled my second cig. "Why did I lose everything?" I thought. "I dunno Jeff – I dunno – but I do care."

With that I put my cig out in the ashtray and slowly went back into the lounge. Some show counting down the best comedy moments was on. I sat back in my chair. Feeling like I didn't really want to be there I tried to watch the TV again.

"Is this Dad again?...I don't think so Jeff – then who – who is it this time? I'm not sure but whoever was helping Dad with the TV two-way mirror broadcasting thingy must have a lot of money to be able to do this. Then who Jeff? ...well who would want you to be happy man? My family? Well yes but they couldn't afford this kind of technology...then who? Jo! Jo's family? Bingo man – they are trying to perk you up Jeff – they could see the fact you left the room and how unhappy you

were...they are trying to help you man! You have it all wrong about Jo's Mum ... and about yesterday – it wasn't next door's daughter that wants to marry you mate – it's Jo!! Well I did propose to her on my birthday last year – well there you go man!"

With that my spirits lifted a bit. I tried to put on a happy face – in fact it wasn't hard by now as I could sense something big was going to happen. How and when I wasn't sure but perhaps through the TV they would let me know the answers.

Well I waited and waited but no face changed to anyone I know. I guess I waited for them to change into either Jo's face or her Mum's but that never happened.

"Ok – so why aren't their faces changing like it did with Dad's? Because they don't need to Jeff – they have employed these people – these comedians. But why would they do that? It can't just be because they have paid them to do this for me...how else then? Well, maybe they are all part of a secret society – like the Masons – they help out other people who are in distress – like you are...look man – look at the TV screen – Ronnie Barker is winking at you now...and this clip is from Porridge...yea so Jeff? Well what are the signs of the

Masons – well castles are one that I know of – yea – and what does the prison look like at the beginning of Porridge – a castle man! There ya go Jeff!"

Before long I was laughing at the TV with a big smile on my face. I wanted to show Jo and her family that it was working. Well it was – my spirits were high and I felt like I was on cloud nine. Before I could get to know what was going to happen – you know the big event – my Mum then changed over for the news.

I always hated the news – depressing stories about war and people being killed and with that thought I nearly left the room for another cig. Yet, for some reason I stayed. It was nearing elections and I wanted to see if the news readers would wink at me also.

"Yep – the two-way TV thingy is working on this channel also – but why would the Masons and Jo want me to vote – and who for? Why is that important? Besides what party should I vote for? Well Jeff – look at the background colour – it's red – they are trying to condition you into voting for the current party in power – Labour. Maybe that's what the news always does – try to get people to vote for the current party in power – remember when the conservatives were in power – the background of the news desk was blue then...you do have a point there Jeff..."

With that I stayed and watched the news about the elections. After it was over the news turned into its usual nastiness so I got up and went for another cig. Before long Mum was calling me in to see the lottery results; "Ahh Jeff – maybe this is it! The big event – go inside and see if we have won!"

"Ok...8, 13, 21, 38, 39, 44...did we win?! Bugger...Well I guess we didn't Jeff – look at Mum's face and your Bro's...never mind Jeff...Jo's family are watching you now – isn't that amazing? You bet ya mate it is..."

I stayed up until my Mum and Bro went to bed and then suggested that I did likewise. "Ok Jeff - time for bed – yea man – that's if I can sleep – well you have to try..." With that I headed upstairs and got into bed. While I replayed the events of the day in mind I couldn't help think of Jo and her family and about the Masonic way...

17

The Castle

After a while I drifted off to sleep however it wasn't long before I was awake again. I needed to go to the toilet so I put on my dressing gown and made my way to the bathroom. After washing my hands I put my hands in my pocket to keep warm. The weather had turned and it was getting cold at nights. "What is that?" I thought as I pulled out a lottery ticket. "I don't remember that being there yesterday – hay man – Jo's family are watching you now – they must have put it there for you! Yes Jeff you have won man!" I could hardly wait to tell my Mum and Bro.

With that I knocked on my Mum's bedroom door and called to my Bro who was sleeping in his attic bedroom upstairs. "We've won – we've won!" I said as Mum came out of her bedroom. "What is it?" she then said as the moonlight reflected the back of her eyes. "Go back to bed" she then said. However, the sight of her eyes – with those cold dark black glistening eyes – then suddenly made me afraid. "She is not herself man – it's night time Jeff and she is still in the underworld – look at her eyes man – you should not have woken her up. Not only that you are jumping the gun – wait till tomorrow. Tell her about the ticket tomorrow. Ok Jeff I will..." I thought as I said I would go back to bed.

After about 15 minutes – I was sure that Mum was asleep. But I couldn't go back to sleep – my mind was racing about the lottery ticket and the fact that Jo could be watching me that second. I decided to go down stairs and get myself a drink. With that I got up and went downstairs – but quietly – I didn't want to wake Mum up again. Standing in the kitchen with the kettle on my attention turned outside and up to the full moon. It was shining on 'the Castle' an old gothic-looking mansion not far from our house. I always thought it had been a church in its past as it had spires and stained glass windows.

I sat at the breakfast bar drinking my tea. I lit a cig and glanced at the clock. It was 3:20am. I noticed that my breathing and heart was beating quite fast at this stage. I kept on looking at the clock – and then at the second hand. I noticed then that the second hand was moving in time with my breaths. "Time is ticking fast tonight" I thought as I consciously tried to slow my breathing down. I had been racing through these past few months – and in the wrong direction – away from Jo, I thought. I had to slow down my life and the best way I could do that was to slow my breathing down. I looked at the clock again and it too seemed to tick by slower. "That's a good sign man – maybe it's rigged up to your heart Jeff – Jo and her family are helping you to slow down your breathing and your life". I then did a test – I held my breath for a few seconds and I swear that the second hand stopped also. "Bingo man – you're spot on!"

I then suddenly realised that tomorrow was Sunday and next door's daughter was getting engaged. But now, however, I knew that it's Jo who wanted to be with me...

"So Jeff – what does that mean then? Well...if Jo wants you then maybe tomorrow you two will be engaged – yes that's it man – the lottery ticket – it's a sign from her! Look at it again...hang on! This is an old ticket from weeks ago – don't you get it man? Jo's family has money – they will give you the

money to live with Jo when you both are engaged – the ticket is only a sign – a promise of this! But wait...not engaged to her Jeff – you did that already on your birthday man – she wants to marry you tomorrow! Fuck me Jeff – it all makes sense now! That's why Dad was helping me get the money – he can't afford to pay for the wedding – he needed your help man! No wonder! ...but where is the wedding going to take place?"

My attention then fell upon the Castle again. "Bingo man – of course it's so obvious now Jeff", I thought; "that's why Mum told me to go back to bed – she is hiding the fact it's tomorrow and that I'll need my rest ...and it's supposed to be surprise. It's going to be a big day tomorrow for you man!"

I was convinced that Jo was nearby – suddenly it dawned on me – Mum didn't go round to next door's to see their daughter – well she'll be there for sure – but to see Jo and meet her family – that's where they have rigged up the monitors and two-way telly broadcasting system and all – it all makes sense now! ... I soon finished my tea. My mind was racing in anticipation and excitement at this point. My gaze then fell onto the row of small terraced houses beyond the back of our garden. They have always reminded me of Grandma's house down south. Almost exactly like it – I thought. I kept on thinking:

"Jeff – Grandma will have to be here for the wedding tomorrow and she would have to have stayed up here over night. So where is she? She's not here that's for sure...Well Jeff think about it...Jo's family are wealthy and with the lottery ticket she could have moved up here...but where? Well she's a traditionalist right? She doesn't like much change...so...so Jeff think about it – the house you are looking at – she must be in one of those houses! My God – yes! That all makes perfect sense now...and...yes? ...what about Dad – he lives or should I say lived in flat – where would he be – well Jeff – how about the block of flats near the Castle? Jeff – that's perfect man! Could it be any more obvious?"

My face had a big smile on it by now. I didn't feel as though I could go back to bed however. "Go find Dad man – go find him. Yea ok man – I know where to look now." With that thought I went upstairs and got changed and came back downstairs – quietly all the time. I then lit a cig for the road and closed the door softly behind me.

Outside the air was cold and I could see my breath as I exhaled. I could sense that Jo or her family watching me from next door as I walked along the road and turned left towards the Castle. As I was walking along I suddenly felt that Dad was trying to communicate with me – perhaps telepathically. As I blinked, suddenly the street lamp came on.

"Dad, what are you trying tell me? Jeff relax – he's saying you are on the right path now...Yea well I wasn't before what with that stupid Ninja bet – yea well he's going to teach you how to be a proper Ninja – a white Ninja tonight. Use your senses and intuition man!"

I walked past another house and tested my senses – I blinked – and low and behold an outside light came on. "Bingo man – he wants you to come and you're going in the right direction – you're going the right way" I thought. Soon I was passing the Castle on my left and headed for the block of flats behind it. As I passed the cars in the car park my eyes fell on a Peugeot. It was a Peugeot 206, a limited edition – I then read the name of it on the back of the car – it said 'The Graduate'.

"Oh my God, Dad knows I love Peugeots... and this one – with the graduate limited edition name is perfect! It's perfectly meant for you Jeff! You are a graduate now man...he's going to give you it tomorrow after the wedding – but shhh it's supposed to be a surprise..."

I carried on walking with a tear rolling down my face. Soon I was standing by the front door of the flats. I looked down and saw someone had some plant pots with plants in them by the front door. "I recognise those pots! They are Dad's" I thought as I made my way inside the building. Once inside I made my way upstairs. I used my intuition about which flat was Dad's. Number 21 – this must be it. He got married to my Mum when he was 21 – it's all falling into place – and I was going to be 21 in a few weeks' time. I then noticed more of the same pots and plants like the ones downstairs. "Your Ninja training is over man – you have made it here" I thought as I rang the doorbell.

After another two rings and no one had answered I felt that my mission that night was the Ninja training but not to see Dad today. With that I made my way home and to bed – I was going to need all the night's sleep – well what was left of it – for tomorrow; my wedding day.

18

The Wedding

Having hardly slept at all I shot up when I heard my Bro coming down the stairs from his bedroom. This was the big day as I looked outside of my window. Cars and more cars were pulling into the Castle's car park. "They are all arriving!" I thought as I made my way into the shower. "Well, I have to look my best" I thought.

Once out of the shower I started to shave. After that I then put on my best aftershave – Cacharel – the one that Dad had given me. I then turned to my wardrobe – "what on Earth could I wear?" I thought as I started sifting through my old clothes I had left in there. I soon came across the old suit my Mum had bought for me for my Grandpa's funeral. "This would be perfect" I thought as I dusted it down. I then picked out a Guinness tie...well, everyone loves the luck of the Irish and you are going to need at the reception I thought as I laid it on the bed. I was beaming; "what a wonderful world it is" I thought as I got into my suit and did up my tie.

"Well here goes" I thought as I started to go downstairs. Mum wasn't up yet and my Bro was already having his breakfast in the lounge watching telly. I then turned on the radio for a briefing.

I heard that it was Jonathan Ross on the radio. I always liked him – his humour and his banter. As I made my breakfast – well I thought I was going to need it today – I then heard Jonathan saying that my favourite comedian – Rik Mayall – was going to be on the show in about a half an hour. "Wow – that can't be a co-incidence" I thought as I poured the milk on my cereal.

"Well Jeff – Jo's family have no expense spared here – they even got you Rik on the radio – based next door – wait, you mean to tell me he's next door?! Well yes man – where else – he's going to be the guest of honour!"

With that thought I could barely eat my cereal I was so excited. I sat and listened for Rik to come on. As I lit a post-breakfast cig and made myself another cup of tea Rik's voice came on loud and clear. Even though he was talking a bit about his accident – which I thought was making fun of my past few months – he said that he was fine now – as I was I thought. He then proceeded to say that he was excited about a new project he was doing in collaboration with some female – the name of who escapes me now. That didn't matter however – he was subtly talking about me and Jo – and I got the innuendos and subtle hints he was dropping my way about my life to date.

Just at the point when I thought he was going to break the charade and say "Welcome to your wedding day Jeff" in walked my Bro. "Bro – you haven't even changed yet man – what the fuck are you doing?" I thought as I lit another cig with my very shaky hands at this point (from excitement you understand).

"Why are you dressed like that" he then said. "That's it" – I thought "fuck we can't keep the guests waiting too long – I need to know what time the wedding is. Perhaps if I bluff him he will tell me". "I'm getting married today and I'm going to call Jo" I said with conviction. "If you do I'll knock you out" came the reply. "So, it's too early" I thought – "ok – I can handle that" as I made my way into the lounge.

Mum then came down stairs. My Bro then had a private word with her – no doubt it was about preparations for the day's events I thought. "See Jeff your Bro said that 'cuz you were about to ruin everything – you have to be patient".

For the next few hours I sat staring at the TV looking for any signs. My Bro was watching the Olympics and I found it difficult to pick up any signs at that point – well apart from winking at the TV when a Brit was performing to help them do well. Apart from going to breakfast bar to have the occasional cig so it remained like this for what seemed like hours.

After getting impatient by that point I glanced at the clock – it was 5 o'clock! "Is this going to be an evening wedding?" I thought. Mum then came in from having been working

in the dining room and suggested that I get out of my suit. That was it – I had to try and call their bluff somehow so I blurted out "but I want to marry Jo today!" "We know you do – but you two have broken up" she then said.

Not really understanding what was going on I went upstairs to take off the suit and tie. "It's too late to fit in the wedding and the reception I thought" as I heard Mum saying that dinner wouldn't be long now. "Fuck dinner" I thought as I threw my tie on the floor but placed my suit carefully back in the wardrobe. After changing into my jeans and jumper I went down stairs and said I was going for a walk. "What about your dinner" Mum then asked me – "save it for me" I said as I closed the door behind me.

19

A Rite of Passage

I needed to be in nature so I headed for the woods. But not the tops wood this time I went for the bottom woods. I was hurt – bitterly hurt as I walked briskly through the rain that was coming down at this point.

As I entered the woods I could feel the rain drops dripping on my face and off my nose. I started breathing heavily as I had been walking briskly. As I was walking – slower this time – I could sense that the trees were swaying with my breath and even the branches were drooping down under the moisture of the rain – but in time with my breath. "Yes man – nature is with you now! Gaia never deserts you man!" I thought as I ventured further into the woods.

Soon I came to an intersection in the path. "This reminds me of the poem by Robert Frost – 'The path less taken' I thought. At which point I thought: "Well Jeff – what path are you going to choose in your life? Are you going to let your family dictate to you your path or are you going to take the path less taken? – well, after today's debacle – I think I will choose that path less taken." My mind then wondered around about how to do that as I stood there at the intersection. I couldn't think straight but I knew I had to choose one path.

"I can't go on with a conscious connection with my parents" I thought as I stood there getting drenched.

"Jeff – you depend too much on both Mum and Dad. And Dad's little trick yesterday on the telly was simply cruel...there's no fuckin' wedding today...and he even led you on the white Ninja training last night...and for what? Absolutely nothing! You need to stop this psychic connection with him man...but how Jeff?"

My attention then started to think about how to ask Gaia and the nature spirits to help me in this endeavor. The trees were still swaying in time to my breath as I then consciously tried to force the psychic connection with my Dad down from my head, past my heart, my waist, my legs and out from the soles of my feet and into the mud at the middle of the intersection. Thunder cracked overhead.

"You are leaving a part of your connection with Dad here at this spot now man – when you walk away from it you must do it mournfully and respectfully...ok Jeff – I understand. But do I really want to do this? Yes you have agreed to man...so finish it..."

With that I started to leave the intersection and take the path less taken. While I took the same path I had taken into the woods back out again it, this time, felt very different indeed. My mind was racing about what exactly I had done but I hope it was going to be for the best.

When I got back home, I took off my muddy shoes and left them by the door. After that I heated up my dinner which had been left for me in the microwave. I only ate half of it – I simply wasn't hungry at all. A few cigs later I took myself to bed – I didn't feel like watching TV anymore that day. I thought I was going to be able to sleep somewhat peacefully after having taken the path I did earlier that evening...I was going to be badly mistaken...

"Dad... psychic power ...intersection... path less taken ...Gaia... cannabis... mushrooms...nature...bad nature...demons...trick...the Devil...death..."

I awoke with the sunlight beaming down on my face. Yet my mind was far from happy... "Dad!!! I have killed you Dad!!!" I burst out crying...

"I didn't know it was a trick – I didn't know it was a demon that tricked me at the intersection last night! I must have performed some kind of ancient – possibly pagan – ritual unwittingly tempted by the Devil – to kill you Dad!!"

With that my Mum came into my room. I blurted out at that I had been tricked and that I had mistakenly killed Dad! She came over and held me saying over and over "it was just a bad dream". It surely was a bad dream I thought – but what I did last night was very very real...I kept on crying...nothing that my Mum said helped at all...I could almost hear my Dad crying with me – full of sadness and pain...I was now crying for two...I thought.

After some time my Mum left the room. I heard her call my Dad on the phone. He lived down south as my Mum and he had divorced when I was about 5-6 years old. More to the point – he was alive!!

20

God Within

With that I got up and went downstairs and into the kitchen. Mum gave me hug and told me that Dad was fine. My Bro had already gone to work so it was just Mum and I for breakfast. Mum then told me that she had also called to make an earlier appointment with Dr Smith – the junior psychiatrist. "Fine with me" I thought as I lit a cig.

After breakfast Mum then asked me to empty the dishwasher. After putting away the plates and silverware I then put the cups and mugs on the stand on the window sill in front of the dishwasher. My attention then turned outside. I could see our pear tree swaying in the breeze and then, suddenly, I remembered about last night. "Will the branches sway with my breath again" I thought as I did a test. To my amazement, they did!

"What could this mean? Well Jeff...you still have the connection with nature and seeing as though you did not unwittingly kill Dad last night – it must be a good connection. Think about it... think about your neural network module at uni man...everything is interconnected...nature must mimic the function of the neurons in the brain...and if the trees sway with your breathing you must be influencing them in some way. Ok Jeff – that makes sense..."

With that thought – Mum said she was leaving for work then. Still thinking about this new theory I had I said nothing. "What about people? How are we all connected?" I thought as Mum left almost drone-like it seemed.

I then picked up a glass from the dishwasher and something amazing happened. The only way I could describe it was that it was akin to the matrix effect I had experienced that day at work in town – but instead of everything turning into the green bits and bytes – I suddenly saw lines of white light connecting everything to – well... everything! Moreover – everything was made of this white light too – but their outlines were still visible.

"I wonder why she didn't say anything...well if what you are seeing is true – then we too are made of the same light...test it man – look at the glass you are holding – look at the trees – now look at your hands man! Oh my God – it's light also! I told ya mate...we are all connected! What is it? I mean – what does this mean? Well – you said it yourself man...God – everything is God – God is the light man!! My God – it's so beautiful! ..."

"But what about the fact that Mum said nothing to me then?...well God is also love man...and do you remember the test you did with the clock in here the other night? Yep – well that wasn't Jo's family's doing – but God's! Love is His fuel for movement man! You did not allow yourself to feel love because of what you thought happened last night – she must have sensed that – God sensed that – and therefore there was no fuel to drive her actions from you man – no fuel to drive her speech...from me? Why from me? Why couldn't she get her fuel from somewhere else man – like the tree? After all she is connected to everything else like I am, no?

...Don't you get it yet man? You are Him! You are God!!! You are the second coming man!!!"

21

'Keep off the Grass'

I stayed in my 'revelation' moment for what seemed like ages. Eager not to forget the connections I saw and made about well, everything and God – I quickly started writing my thoughts down. I also surmised that the drugs that I took with Steve and Co. – i.e. the cannabis, E and mushrooms – was the Devil's way of stopping God's light and love – flowing through me. All this I wrote down. Before lunch I had written about 20 pages of the little booklet I had found to write in. Entitled 'Keep off the Grass' – it was quickly turning into a masterful and insightful piece of work which had to be shared I thought.

In fact by the time Mum and my Bro had returned home from work I was still writing. I explained it away to them as notes about my thoughts I would share with Dr. Smith when I next saw her. "That's tomorrow" my Mum then told me. I didn't care about that as I was on a high – a natural, divine high – by this point.

Not being afraid I then sat in the lounge to eat dinner with my Mum and Bro. There were no winking or face changes that occurred this time. I was somewhat relieved of that I must say. "If only I could tell them about me and what happened today" I thought as my Bro started channel hoping. "Well you are – with your journal – but that can wait."

That night I found new respect for both my brother and mother. My Bro was studying to be a teacher and Mum already was one. "I have a wonderful family" I thought as I thought about my life's journey to date and how they both have taught me so many things – all to help me get to this realisation point – I thought. To be taught by God through them to see Himself – to see myself in them – the ultimate teacher of life. How can God realise himself without a mirror? I thought. Without another to reflect His image back at Himself – to reflect His love back at Himself?

The next day I went to my appointment with Dr. Smith on a high. To be honest I don't remember what I said to her – but whatever it was – I left feeling happy, loved and so alive. Things, however, were going to change...my last thought during these days was:

How can God know Himself if he doesn't have His opposite? From then onwards – my mind goes blank...as did 'Keep off the Grass'...

22

A & E

PART TWO: ...To the Mine

I have no memory of the days between 1st and 7th of November 2000 at all. Whatever occurred, whatever I said or did must have seemed erratic, illogical and frightening for both my Mum and brother. What is certain, however, was that I too must have been finding living and coping both difficult and frightening also. My family's concern became overtly apparent as, on the night of the 8th, my Mum made several phone calls asking for advice and ultimately, I suspect, help.

Before I had time to process what was going on I was being driven down to A & E. It was about seven or eight-ish at night. I, by now, really hated being out after six o'clock. The whole way there I pleaded for them to take me back home. I couldn't stop shaking and I had to concentrate hard on my breathing. I remember my brother doing his best to try and calm me down while suggesting I just enjoy the ride. "Enjoy?" I thought, "How can I possibly enjoy it?" Everywhere I looked outside people were looking in our direction or talking on their mobiles. "Yeah, they knew who I was, what I had done, no way is this bastard getting away *that* easily."

I looked down at my shoes the rest of the way after that. I couldn't tell my Mum and Bro what I knew and what I had done for their sake. I felt alone to face the music by myself, and it seemed like it was coming sooner rather than later. Even though it was now full of bad memories, demons, and cursed objects, home seemed like the safest place to be. They knew where I lived alright, as I had remembered by now that Vince and Jim came to collect me when I was moving out, but so far they hadn't made their move just yet. "Perhaps they needed me away from my family in order to do so. Well, they got me right where they want me now", I thought as we turned into the multi-storey car park.

Once inside the car park my thoughts then turned to Grandpa; "Mum has always told you Jeff that your Bro is very like your Grandpa. Stay close to him – they will both help you now man..."

Once we had found our way from the car park to A & E all three of us went inside. My Mum then went up the reception desk to get me seen. My Bro and I however sat down on some of the plastic waiting chairs. The TV was on in one corner and there was a football match on. Who was playing I couldn't tell you as my mind was focused heavily on my breathing and I was watching the front door in case we had been followed.

"Do you think we were followed Jeff? Well it's possible...I mean I did see a few scouts and spies for them as we drove down here – they know where you are now. They are just waiting till you are alone – then they'll grab ya man...stay close to your Bro – he'll look out for you...Ok, I will Jeff..."

Before too long my number had been called. My Bro stayed sitting watching the football match as my Mum and I went into a cubical for assessment. I wanted my Bro to come with us too but for some reason I couldn't or didn't say that. As we sat there I could see past the curtains into the area beyond where I could see people moving about. All of a sudden a man walked past my vision and his face morphed into my Dad's face. He was standing near what looked like a bed with a 50 something year old woman lying in it.

"Why is Dad here? ...He's here to look out for you man – and help clean up the mess you have caused... but what mess? You know perfectly well Jeff – by getting Jo involved in drugs you have drained her Mum of her energy – that's who Dad is looking after now – back there...in that bed. And by getting your-self involved in that drug cult you have unwittingly performed black magic by using the drugs you got from them and don't forget the ritual you did at the intersection in the

woods...selling your soul to the Devil – you remember? You are in league with him now!! Fuck no way! I didn't mean to do that! Well man – it's too late now – there's only one way out..."

After a few minutes the on-call junior psychiatrist came in to assess me. All I was thinking at this point was a way out of the shit I was in. "What was the one way out?" I thought as Mum recounted the story and how I came to be at A & E. I didn't feel in league with the Devil – but possessed by the drugs maybe in some form which has caused and is causing me to drain energy from those I love. It had to stop and now. "But how can I make it stop Jeff? Well man – if you are possessed – you need an exorcism". With that the junior doctor then turned to me and asked me how I was feeling now. "I need help. I want an exorcism" I said in desperation.

With that he got out a little torch and turned it on to look in my eyes. He then asked me to look at the light as he moved it from right to left and then up and down.

"This is it Jeff – the beginning of the exorcism! He just asked you to look into the light, urging you to return to the light man and then made the sign of the cross with it! You got your wish – thank God!"

My Mum then suggested that I go and wait with my Bro while she and the doctor had a talk about something. "Fine with me" I thought. I found my Bro outside having a cig. "Good idea" I thought as I rolled myself one too and lit up. "What did the doctor say to you?" my Bro then asked me. I couldn't remember much of what was said, only the fact that my exorcism had started. "I'm being saved" I replied.

It wasn't long before Mum came out to join us. She then turned to me and said that she and the doctor both thought it was a good idea for me to go into hospital. "I don't need to go, I don't want to go Mum" I then said. "It will be alright" my Bro then said trying to reassure me.

After a few cigs later I realized that I was fighting a losing battle trying to convince my Mum and Bro that I didn't need to go. I then saw an ambulance pull up and Mum went inside reception for a moment. When she came out she said that the ambulance was for me. She re-assured me that everything would be ok and that she would come with me in the ambulance and that my Bro would follow us in the car. "That's something at least" I thought.

I was admitted to St. Michael's Hospital psychiatric wing on the 8th of November 2000.

23

The First Night

Once inside the psychiatric wing all three of us were escorted to the ward. I was then asked by one of the staff members on the ward to go into the main office and see the duty doctor for admission. "Fuck this – I don't want to be admitted here" I thought as he started to take my blood pressure and pulse. "Jeff – just relax mate – I know you don't want it – so just relax your breathing and pulse and he will see that everything is normal. Ok man – I will try that." After he had taken both my blood pressure and pulse he went outside to talk to both my Mum and Bro. "Why didn't he ask me to go with him? What is he saying to them" I thought as I sat there.

When the doctor finally opened the door Mum and my Bro were standing in the corridor. "Please don't leave me here!" I said "they will fucking get me in here, I just know it" I thought. After a few minutes of reassurance and saying that they will be back to visit, my Mum and Bro left.

One of the staff members then called me to the medicines counter to take a pill of some kind. I have no idea what kind it was, perhaps a sedative, in hindsight I now believe. She then ushered me into the dormitory where twenty beds, ten on each side, were lined up in a row with curtains around them. And there she left me; with a bed a small cupboard/bedside table and a small wardrobe. Some hospital issue pyjamas and slippers were laid out on the bed. I pushed them all off the bed – got undressed and got into the bed with my boxers on as normal.

"No fucking way am I wearing those clothes...they aren't mine...and what...the fuck...is that noise? It sounds like horses naying and snorting! Is this the nature voodoo returning?? Well Jeff...it's not like you don't deserve it man..."

Thoughts of wild beasts; half horse and half monster – almost chimera-like with perhaps griffin wings and lion bodies but with the sound of horses filled my mind. I could see the curtains move with the beat of their wings as terror started to set in.

I couldn't get to sleep for what seemed like hours; not with all those noises and images in my mind going on about me. After what seemed like hours, however, I eventually fell into a restless night's sleep.

24

The Last Great Trick

Something had disturbed my sleep, or rather what little I had that night. As I opened my eyes I saw that someone was at the foot of my bed saying that it was breakfast time. With that I slowly got up somewhat dazed and lethargic from whatever pill I had taken the night before. By now I had no clue where I was or what I was supposed to do.

As I slowly pulled back my curtain surrounding my bed I could see several males walking around in a state of a kind of zombie-like trance. I could also see a man in the bed opposite me reading a newspaper. The title headline was 'My dreams have come true.' "Where the fuck am I?" I thought as I heard someone open the door to the dormitory and walk towards my cubical. They then asked me to follow them and then showed me the shower room.

"I need to take a shower then huh? Well ok but I'm not getting anywhere near that mirror – I know your game – I know this trap. Jeff – if they get you to look in the mirror then they will know where you are man! They will get you! Well that just isn't going to happen..."

With that I closed the door behind me and scooted down past the mirror so as not to catch a glimpse of myself in it.

Once in the shower I turned the water on. It was hot – scalding even. I tried turning it down but to no effect.

"This is it Jeff – the end – you have betrayed God and Jesus...just fucking die! I know you feel it coming so do it...Ok so you want a rundown of your life then huh? Ok here goes:... shit shit and more shit! Satisfied?!"

With that thought I raced through my mind for all my life's memories – and to say that I got close to all of them would be a good approximation of it....time sped up and I died mentally several times..."What the fuck do you want from me??" I screamed as I had let go of myself and my life.

Yet I was still there. I then got the distinct feeling that everything was pre-destined and out of my control. It was bound to end up this way I thought.

"You have no control over your own destiny now Jeff – you have given that privilege away man! You are now the property of the Devil!"

I had a distinct feeling that the Devil was nearby and I started praying to God as the water rained down on my head and down my body. This was his last great trick – you cannot die when you have sold your soul to him. You can try – but that is part of your torture.

I then began to say the Lord's Prayer in desperation, well what I knew of it:

"Oh Lord Hallowed be thy name. Thy Kingdom come thy will be done on Earth as it is in Heaven. Give us this day our daily bread and forgive our trespasses as we forgive those who have trespassed against us. And lead us not into temptation. For thyne is the kingdom, the power and glory...oh Lord

please help me now!! Jeff – what is that man doing saying he has stolen your dreams? He must be the Devil – project your love and prayers at him!!!"

"You have wasted your dreams and energy on drugs – and now it's his turn to take them!" My mind then turned to my Mum who had said that she would be a Godmother to my best friend's sister while I was at primary school. While their family was a Christian family my Mum said that she would be a Godmother to her only in principle as she had problems with the Bible and Christian Faith in general.

"Who was this man?" I thought as I was singing the Lord's Prayer at him – over and over again in the shower. "Maybe he is my best friend's Dad" I thought – it was always a bit hazy about who he was and where he was from. Either way – I loved my friend and his family and I wanted to make amends as best I could – to him, his sister (on my mother's behalf) and to his father. I sang and prayed and pointed my hands in his direction; yet nothing seemed to change.

After a while I got out of the shower, got myself dry and got changed and went to have breakfast.

25

A Name to a Place

Once in the dining room I got myself some cereal. I sat down at a table and began to eat. When I had finished eating my breakfast I then had a look at a newspaper that was lying around the dining room. I could make no sense of it what so ever. It was as if the words were the wrong way round in the sentences – back to front if you like. I knew it was English but it made no sense to me at all.

I then read the health and safety sign in the corridor and again it made no sense to me. Again in the small beverage area there was a sign about making toast and the fire brigade.

"What the fuck is this all about...toast cost 4p a slice and then it costs £900.04 and the fire brigade comes? What the fuck is it trying to tell me? Why is nothing making any sense? Well Jeff...you haven't worked out where you are, have you yet? Don't you get it? Do you hear that buzzing in your ear? ...it sounds like a wasp...yes that's because you are afraid of them...this whole place is slowly changing into what you are afraid of...bit by bit things will change into meaningless states of reality Jeff...it's your worst nightmare come true...it's making you think that you are going insane...you have no control over it man. Soon I will be insane! So where is this place then? Think of it like your worst

idiosyncratic nightmare man...all your worst fears will become manifest in this place. Welcome to Hell Jeff!"

At that moment a man dressed in priestly black robes and wearing a white collar walked past me and went into a room along the corridor. "Has he come to read me my last rites?" I thought.

"Well Jeff...you still have one foot in this reality man...but slowly – surely – you will be surgically removed from this reality – from this space and time - and more and more you will be placed in that reality man...which one? Hell Jeff! This is your decent into Hell! You have betrayed God by selling your soul to the Devil and now you will be punished and tortured for all eternity."

"On Earth as it is in Heaven...yes well not for you anymore...you are going downstairs Jeff! And the good Lord God will strike you down soon man...But how? Well you know that God is the light and through light he will strike you down! You mean the sun? Yes man...that is a reflection of His power in this reality...beware of the sun Jeff for your time has come!"

For several hours I wandered around the ward getting used to my new surroundings. No matter who I talked to or what I read I could not shake off the fear that had started to set into me as a result of what I believed was happening to me. While trying to keep out of the direct sunlight streaming in from the windows, I suddenly noticed that a large majority of people on the ward were wearing black. "Why is everyone wearing black? Well Jeff, in this world you are dead man...and they are all going to your funeral... that's why you saw the priest earlier."

With that thought I then heard someone saying it was lunch time. I slowly made way back into the dining room and lined up to get some lunch. I then chose a table which was out of the direct sunlight and began to eat. When I was about half the way through my meal I heard the familiar sounds of keys rattling and in walked my Mum. I was ex-tremely happy to see her but not to see the fact that she too was wearing black. "Well Jeff – your Mum is also at your funeral now – but only a part of her – by the grace of God – has been allowed to come and say a final goodbye to you...Help me Mum! Please!! Get me out of here!!"

I pleaded with her to take me home as one of the staff members came and sat at our table. She replied to my pleading with comments like "it's for the best that you stay here" and "everything is going to be ok". Mum then asked the staff member how I was doing and then told me to finish eating. "Have your lunch" she said. Lunch was the last thing on my mind however I started to get some of the peas on my plate onto my fork.

"See Jeff – even your Mum says that it's best that you stay here – in Hell – she knows what you have done to deserve this now...She is with God and the rest of the world...and they are all against you..."

I felt so ashamed and scared that I could not look up from my plate by now. I could feel the sun's rays intensifying as a beam of light shone on the table close to my plate and right past my head. "Shit – this is it – I'm going to die here and now and the transformation into Hell will begin in earnest" I thought and said... "I'm so sorry Mum...I'm so sorry!"

"It doesn't matter now" she said. "See! She knows where you are going and what you have done and there is nothing you can do about it!" I continued to stare at the centre of my plate. There was a rural scene printed on the bottom of it which reminded me of Jo and of her Mum and my aunty. Thoughts about the Night of the Long Knives came flooding back to me as I said "I'm so sorry" over and over again. At that moment the sun's ray then fell on my plate. "Fuck – please no! I'm so so sorry God!" I thought. I couldn't look up or do anything – I was paralysed with fear – so I continued to stare at the centre of the plate. The gravy left on my plate then started to sparkle like stars in the Heavens from the sun's ray falling on it. "Here goes Jeff...are you ready for it? Are you ready to meet the Devil?" Tears started to pour down my face as all I could think of was Jo and my family...

26

The Mark of the Beast

Mum then said she was going to leave me now. "It has started" I thought as she hugged me and walked out of the dining room. "You'll never see her again now Jeff..." The staff member then asked if I would like to have a talk with one of my workers. The next thing I knew I was being ushered into a room with a male staff member called Eric. He had dark skin and long black hair. My attention then focused on his forehead where a scar was. It looked to me like it was in the shape of a swastika or Buddhist eternity symbol.

"That's right Jeff – you are right – he is a demon come to start your torture. You see that mark on his forehead? It denotes evil and the length of the evil – eternity man...well, I'm not going to give him the satisfaction of that. I'm not going to talk to him – or anyone here from now on...see how they like that! In fact, I'm leaving..."

With that I got up and left the room. I knew where the entrance to the ward was so I made a b-line for it, hoping that no one would notice me. I went down stairs and out through what I thought was the entrance only to find myself in a walled rose garden. I could see a gate in the wall but before I could get to it Eric was standing behind me calling my name. I turned around but said nothing. He told me that I couldn't leave the ward and suggested that we had a chat back up there. My escape had been rumbled I thought, "but I can try another time".

Once back on the ward he led me back to the same room we were in earlier. This time he left me there for a few minutes. My mind then started to think about the Devil and how he tricks people into selling their souls.

"You know why you are here...but how did he trick me? He tempted you man and you took his bate...the weed Jeff – it's a gateway into his realm – that's how he

sources his conscripts...that's why it's illegal man...the government knows this and is fighting a war with the Devil and so is the Queen, as God's messenger by divine authority...You are like Judas who took the bait man – who gave in to temptation."

With that I thought about the Night of the Long Knives again and about how I was going to end up in London beheaded by the Queen. I suddenly felt a strong presence in the room as I glanced over at the chair where Eric had been sitting in earlier. There was a dark shadow in the form of an elderly lady 'sitting', I thought, in the chair.

"You know who that is, don't you Jeff? Is it...? Yes Jeff – it's Her Royal Highness the Queen...and you know why she is here don't you...for me? Yes – she has the ability to project her spirit into this realm and behead the fallen ones – and you Jeff have performed dark magic and are in league with the Devil – she has to banish you to Hell now...kneel! Kneel down before her Jeff! Do it now!"

I slowly went down on one knee and lowered my head – ashamed and humble before her. "Do you know what she is going to do to you now Jeff? Behead me? That's right! It's no more than you deserve!"

With that thought Eric walked back in and asked why I was kneeling on the ground. "Just get it over with" I thought as the slow realization that this was all part of the trick - all part of the scam and torture of Hell dawned on me. Sometimes the anticipation of pain and death is worse than the actual thing itself. "This is a mind-fucker" I thought. "Well Jeff – you are in Hell after all – do you want some more?"

I slowly got up and went into the smoking room. I needed a cig and badly. My hands were shaking and tobacco was falling on the floor as I tried to roll my cig. Once finally rolled and lit my mind started to race around thinking of ways to make amends with the Queen and ultimately with God. As I was thinking my attention started to focus on the pictures people had done and had stuck on the smoke room wall. I then noticed one of them stood out as it had some writing underneath it. I took it off the wall and started to read what was written...

Dark Angels

You are troubled by your dark angels...
You seek to tame their wildness...
But they are the potential source of creativity within you...
If you deny them, banish them, seek to destroy them, they will
drain you of passion as they retreat,
and you will become pale and lifeless...
And if they should return and storm your gates, you would then be
destroyed...
However dark, they are still angels, guardians and protectors too...

"Read it Jeff – read it aloud... again ...and again louder! ...again ...again! Keep doing it until you truly repent for your sins Jeff! And you better fucking mean it this time!!"

I sat in the smoke room saying this poem over and over again as loudly as I could until tears started to roll down my face. I was rocking back and forth as I read in desperation.

27

Confession

How long I stayed sitting and rocking back and forth while reading the poem over and over again I have no idea. It felt like an eternity. When I did eventually stop my thoughts then turned to confession. I needed to confess to someone but not to anyone here. I need to confess via the proper channels. "Perhaps the police station in town is still there in this reality" I thought as I looked outside the window. It was dusk and starting to get dark. "If you go now you might get there before its 6 o'clock man." With that I got up and walked towards the exit of the ward.

This time, luckily, no one saw me. I then knew which way was the entrance to the building through the process of elimination from my trip to the rose garden earlier. Before I knew it I was running out of the building and out into the hospital grounds. I wasn't very sure of where I was but by the cityscape I had a rough idea which direction town was. I kept on running in that direction. Feeling like I was being watched or followed by the cars on the road I changed sides of the pavement several times but kept on running.

"Hurry up Jeff! You're not going to make it before 6 at this rate! Look

I'm going as fast as I can! Do you remember the car brake lights equating to your Bro? Well they don't anymore – they are the Devil's eyes watching you man...he knows what you are trying to do but it won't work...yea well we'll see about that..."

With that thought I entered the outskirts of town. While it looked somewhat different from what I was used to I nevertheless still knew where I was and in which direction the police station was.

Before too long I was standing outside the main police station in town. I wasted no time and went inside. I approached the main desk and said that I would like to make a confession. I was then told to sit and wait and someone would be by to see me. After about 5 minutes two police officers came to me and the three of us went into what seemed like a small interview room. "Ok Jeff – tell them – go on – tell them what you have done." I started off by telling them I want to confess to smoking cannabis. They then asked me a few questions like when the last time I had used it and where I had got it from. I then proceeded to ask if I had been saved therefore. They both then looked at each other. "Where do you live?" came the reply. I gave them my Mum's address. He then left the room as the remaining police officer asked if I wanted a cup of coffee. "Coffee? At a time like this?" I thought but replied yes to it anyway. I was thirsty from the long run I had just done.

After about 5 minutes I had my coffee. It tasted good and hot. "Just what I need" I thought as I heard the other officer come back in the room. "Well Sir, I have just spoken with your mother and I have arranged for someone to take you back to hospital." "I don't want to go back there" I thought, "it's Hell" I said in desperation. But maybe – just maybe it will be different now that I have confessed I thought.

While I don't remember being driven back to the hospital I do remember, upon returning back to the ward, Eric asking me why I had left and asked me not to do it again. I remained silent.

28

Can I have a Light?

Several days had passed and I was still fearful. I had spent most of my time in the smoke room with the other 'inmates' as they called themselves. I was very anxious that something was going to happen to me or the world during this time. While I kept silent for those days I had been listening and absorbing what my fellow inmates had said. One person, in particular, seemed to know something about aliens and UFOs and reading people's minds it seemed. That got me to thinking about the UFO I saw when I was with Vince. "How did that fit into all of this?" I thought. My mind was racing by now.

"Well Jeff you know that the government covers up UFO sightings...so they must be hiding a secret. Ok yea – but what? Well first of all they are either the work of God or...or? Or the Devil man. And this is Hell...so they must be the work of the Devil – for this is his realm you are in now. And the government knows that they are the work of the Devil ...But what do the aliens want? Well what does the Devil want? He wants the end of the world man! That's the impending disaster that you are feeling now Jeff!"

"But how is it going to happen? Well that girl over there says the aliens can read people's minds...yea so? So, if they can, all they need to do is slowly

take over the people's mind and bodies...but they will need energy won't they? Yes of course man, they are coming to get the energy of the sun Jeff! They want to drain the energy of the sun...but they need its exact coordinates...but won't God stop them? Well He's trying to Jeff – but all it needs is one person to give the coordinates away to the aliens through their thoughts then it is game over man! ...but wait, surely the aliens can't understand our language can they? Well no – but they are

learning to...well how do you tell if someone's possessed by aliens then? Is there some kind of way of telling that?..."

As I sat there rocking out of fear I heard a voice speak up: "Can I have a light?" I slowly looked up and lit my lighter. Then it dawned on me: "the aliens are after God Himself – the light – the sun – the aliens and the Devil are in league with each other – they are really one and the same thing man!!" Can I have a light? Is their way, their code, for saying show me, in your mind, the coordinates of the Sun – our Father! – Lord God Himself!

"Jeff whatever you do – don't think about the sun – why do you think I'm possessed by aliens man? Well you certainly are possessed by the Devil now – so I guess there's your answer! Shit Fuck – stop thinking about our galaxy, our solar system – our sun! FUCK!!! FUCK YOU JEFF! GAME OVER you have just given away the sun's location – it's game over now man! Well done, our sun is God and you have killed Him man – it's only a matter minutes now and the sun will start to grow cold. You have brought the end of Heaven on Earth and have opened the gates to Hell on Earth!! ...but wait!! I didn't mean to!! Tough shit now man – it's all over – and all thanks to you! You and your weak resolve towards temptation!"

I could almost hear people outside crying and weeping for the end was nigh and I knew it was my entire fault. Even the people around me in the smoke room knew it was me who had just caused the end of the world and I couldn't stand it. I couldn't stand myself. With that I threw my cig in the ashtray and went into the dining room looking for a knife. There were none. I grabbed a fork instead and went straight into the toilets and locked the door behind me. "Go on Jeff – do it – you might as well" I then stabbed myself in the stomach with the fork. Barely going in at all I grabbed the silver chain around my neck and pulled it as hard as I could. I couldn't breathe but that was not my intention.

Soon the power of my grab weakened as I looked down at the sink. Lying there was my shaver. I picked it up switched it on and pressed as hard as I could into my face. I just wanted to die there and then – I realized the futility of my actions however as I was already dead in reality – but that didn't stop me.

Realizing that the shaver did nothing also – I put it down and with my nails I dug into my face and pulled the skin apart. As I looked up I faced the mirror for the first time since being there. Blood was by now running down my cheeks – I didn't recognize myself at all.

Then came a knock at the door and someone said to let them in. I was terrified of who or what would be standing there now that Hell had been unleashed onto the world.

29

Sins of the Father

It was Eric. "Not that fucking demon again" I thought as he took the fork off of me. He then told me that I will be moved into the small room by myself along the corridor. He told me to get my things from the dormitory and follow him. Once inside the room he told me that someone will be right outside the door at all times and to go to sleep. "Keeping a closer eye on me huh?" I thought as laid down on the bed.

To say that that night's sleep was the worst night's sleep I had ever had would be a serious understatement. For starters I felt like every 30 minutes or so someone would watch me through the door's glass window. "They are really doing their job these demons" I thought. Secondly, the sleep I did get I did not really sleep. Instead, I relived the day's events over and over and over again. It was as if I did not sleep at all.

A few days went by and to my astonishment Mum came to visit me again. She was still wearing that long black coat so I was very suspicious, "is this another trick?" I thought.

"Fuck you Devil – I might have unwittingly helped you to bring about the

end of the world but you are not going to take my sanity too! I know this isn't Mum – you'll have to do better than that!"

I stayed silent throughout her visit much to her dismay and worry no doubt.

Slowly I realized that not talking wasn't getting me anywhere. I was still in Hell I thought. They are still tormenting me – the Devil and his demons – that won't change. But something inside me had shifted somehow. Slowly but surely I started to talk again.

The next contact I got was a phone call from my Dad. His voice sounded odd and strange to me. Convinced it wasn't him either there were long pauses between my words...

"If this is Hell then this wouldn't be Dad – no, it's him - the Devil! You mean to say they are one and the same? That's right Jeff! How do you like Hell now? Your Dad is the Devil...which makes you...any guesses? The anti-Christ? Bingo! Fun isn't this? Welcome to your Hell Jeff! All of this is you and your Dad's fault and doing! Then who is the second coming? Well your Bro and you have different Dads – think about it – he won and you lost man!! Gets better doesn't it?"

Everywhere I looked I could see demons and shadows. Even when seeing the 'junior doctor' I could see dark shadows sitting on the chairs next to him. They were lighting up cigarettes – mocking me about how I had helped their master – the Devil – to take over the world.

The next time my 'Mum' came to visit me I asked her about her and Dad and how they got married. I found out that Dad had gotten married to my Mum when he was 21, just like me in about ten days' time. I also asked her about Grandma's religion – Methodism – and what it means. I was desperately still seeking a way out of my own private Hell.

30

Arc Angel

Thoughts carried on in this vein until one day we had a new 'inmate' on the ward. I saw him being wheeled in a wheelchair past the smoke room and into the dormitory. He had plaster cast on his lower left leg I noticed. "He must be in bad shape" I thought for he did not move out of bed for two days straight. "Is he dying too?" A woman sat by his bedside for those two days until finally he got up and wheeled himself into the smoke room on the third day late at night. I couldn't sleep and so, it seemed, like half the male dormitory.

As we huddled in that smoke filled room I listened to Ray, as was his name, talking with another inmate. I heard Ray say that he was a light-worker. My ears literally pricked up. "Ray works with light then huh?" I thought as he started to tell his story of how he came to be in here with us.

"Perhaps he has come to help save us – perhaps he is an undercover light worker from God...what was that he just said? He lost his eye? He shot it? Oh my God! He must have been fighting with some heavy duty demons for him to want to do that...the best you could do Jeff was to choke and gauge yourself. What was that – he uses his third-eye chakra to project love and light out

from? Perhaps you are right Jeff...perhaps he has been sent by God – but he still smokes cigarettes ...be careful man."

I stayed sitting there listening to Ray talk about when he has a cigarette he says a blessing and makes a request for the world. I then started to strike up conversation with Ray. We talked for what seemed like hours. "This guy is helping to save the planet – perhaps this Ray of light – this Ray Gunn – this Ray Cyclops – really could be helping to turn things around for the world. I wonder if he could do the same for me.

By the next day I was starting to feel a bit calmer but emotionally I had given up. I also wasn't sure what the state of the world was in outside. In addition I had been moved back into the dormitory along with the other inmates; yet this time to a different bed near the door. At nights I used to lie on my bed and listen to the local pirate radio station with reggae and Rasta tunes playing. One night I remember thinking that if I really concentrate I might be able to stop my heart just by thinking about it. At that moment Clare – my keyworker demon – came in and sat on my bed. She was attractive looking with long dark hair. As I had been crying she asked me what the matter was. "I miss my family" I simply said. We then had a talk that, to my surprise, actually made me feel a bit better. I still knew I was in Hell – but I was getting used to it by now.

After she left I sat there looking at the moon through the window. Its rays shone down onto the floor and I swear to you – there lying on the floor – was the sign of the Cross. "Maybe all is not lost" I thought as I smiled and went to sleep.

The next day another new inmate had come in. His name was Michael. I had noticed that he had a jacket and on the back of it were the words 'Arc Angel'. I made friends with Michael quickly. I had a funny feeling that something was turning for me. While Michael was prone to anger at times he was a very gentle soul I thought. He reminds me of the Arc Angel Michael – the angel of the north – who fights the dragons and demons for God. My thoughts then turned to the outside world "I wonder how it's doing – is it really Hell out there – or not?"

I was soon going to find out. A few days later Michael came into the smoke room and asked if I would like to go for a walk with him outside. I replied that I did. I was very nervous and anxious about being outside for not only was I scared about how it might look but also about being in the sunlight still.

Yet once outside the sunlight was shining brightly and fell softly on my face. I trod carefully and respectfully knowing that I had offended Gaia and God. "Where would you like to go?" Michael then asked me with a grin. "Is there a church near here do you know?" I then replied. "Yes man – there's one here in the hospital grounds."

With that we made our way slowly to the church. Once inside I could see a piano and the pews. At the far end was a pulpit and a cross in shiny gold. Michael walked right up to the Cross and at that exact moment a ray of brilliant light fell on his head. "Jeff man – did you see that!? I surely did! In fact – check out those too man!" All about us I could see small balls of flashing light. I then asked Michael if he was a Christian – to which he replied that he was.

31

The Abbey

Going to the church with Michael soon became a bit of a habit. While I didn't see any more balls of light, I did, however, speak to the priest there to let me use the piano from time to time. I used to have piano lessons when I was younger. Even though I couldn't remember hardly any of it I could play the beginning to Fur Elise which I enjoyed playing.

Soon after that, the day came when I was due for my first trip outside the hospital grounds. I was both excited and nervous at the same time. I had spoken with my Mum the day before and she asked me where I would like to go. Well seeing as though it was Sunday today and the weather looked nice, I thought a trip out to the old Gregorian Abbey not too far from the city might be a day out I would enjoy.

Mum then came to pick me up from the ward around 11ish. We had a bit of a drive ahead of us and we were going to stop for lunch at a little bistro restaurant not too far away from the old abbey. The drive there was fairly smooth even though I was still a bit anxious being away from the now familiar surroundings of the ward and the few friends I had made there. Most of the way there we were talking about faith in general and then about what the Methodists believe in. This, I suspect, was from my prompting.

We then stopped off to have some lunch at the little bistro restaurant. Once inside it quickly became apparent that everyone and their uncle wanted lunch there as it was Sunday and it was a very popular place to eat. That being said we didn't have to wait too long to be seated. The meal was good and tasty and soon we were on our way across the fields of sheep headed towards the abbey on foot. "Boy is it great to be out in nature again" I thought as we walked past the sheep and near the river that flowed gently to our right.

"Gaia, I'm so sorry for what I thought I had done to you...and for abusing your secrets...I guess in the wrong or rather untrained and unprepared hands it can be potentially disastrous...I know that now. I respect you more now than I have ever done before and I hope you know that."

Before too long we were coming up to the old abbey. Children were playing in the river with their parents looking on. After looking around the old abbey for a while I then suggested that we went into the old church attached to the abbey that was still in use, even to this day I think. Sensing Mum's unease about this suggestion I reassured her that not only will I be fine but she also.

Once inside the church we were struck by the most beautiful and melodic Gregorian chanting I have ever heard. While I looked around to see who was singing I saw no one. "It must be a tape" I then said to Mum. At the back of the church were some books and trinkets which we looked at and then started to look around the church going round in a circle from left to right. At one point we came across a donation box. I fumbled around for some change and dropped it in. "Thank-you, Lord, for a nice day" I then said in my mind as the coins fell from my hands.

After looking at the rest of the church we made our way back to the car parked in the car park of the restaurant. On the way home I pointed out to Mum a brilliant full rainbow high up in the sky.

"God's Covenant...who is that for? Well traditionally for all of humanity Jeff – ok yea, but right now I feel like it's for me and for me alone. Well man – you might be right there – you just might be right..."

The next day Ben, my old housemate whilst at uni, came to visit me. I was really happy to see him and I suggested we had a game of chess. Obviously, this reminded me of my Grandpa, which brought back warm happy memories this time. Then also, before I knew it,

Jo's housemates also came to visit me. This uplifted me but I was saddened to see that Jo herself was not with them. "Does she not care about me anymore? Does she not want to see me – just as friends to see how I am doing?" After talking with her housemates I was told she knew where I was but that she was too upset at the moment and needed some time alone. "Fair enough" I thought. It then dawned on me why I was getting these visits. My birthday was the following day as they all had come bearing gifts. What with one thing and another, my birthday had completely slipped my mind.

On the day of my 21st birthday I was pleasantly surprised to see that not only my Mum and Bro had come to visit me but also my Grandma had made the long trip up from the south of the country to be here. I was truly touched. We all went into the lounge. Mum or Grandma had brought a cake for me. "We can't eat all of it" I thought so I invited in Ray, Michael and another inmate called Ruth with whom I had been getting on well with into the lounge with us to enjoy the cake and the celebrations.

I only remember one gift from that birthday. Perhaps the best gift apart from seeing my family again and together was a sketchbook and some colouring pencils my Mum had given me. "If you ever feel like not talking again – then draw" she said with a smile.

That night I started to sketch how I would like my bedroom back at Mum's to be when I got out of there. Ruth was sitting on the couch opposite me and who wants to be a millionaire was on TV.

"Ok Ruth – I know this game – do you? We can help this contestant win by how we blink our eyes at the correct answer. There you go – that's it...boy I love how you twitch your nose – it's so cute!"

That night I drew, twitched my nose at Ruth, and helped Judith Keppel become the first winner of who wants to be a millionaire. "Good for her!" I thought with a beaming smile across my face.

32

I Can, I Will & I'm Gonna!

After my birthday my spirits were rising. I attended each and every group on the ward that was offered to me. At this point an occupational therapist was assigned to me and we discussed what groups I would like to attend down in the OT department. I chose the art group, confidence building, wood work and pottery. I also started going for coffee with her in the unit's canteen once a week. OT was a Godsend for me during this period and the technical instructor was pushing my creativity to the max. I loved every minute of it.

While in the OT department I also had the opportunity to mix with other 'inmates' from other wards. Ruth was also attending many of my groups or else I found myself spending a lot of time with her, as well as Michael and Ray.

"Do you like this girl Jeff? Well yes I do – I must confess I do...Well what about Jo? I'm not sure...well you did propose to her man...I know I know...I need to see Jo again if I can – meet her face to face and see if we both still feel the same or not...Are you kidding man? She left you! I know that man...but if my heart is still with Jo I cannot pursue anything with Ruth until I know – one way or the other..."

Things progressed in this vein until one day I attended a group on the ward called 'Aims and Objectives'. It was a goal setting group and I had an idea of what goal I would like to achieve. I had called Jo the day before and she had agreed to meet me in town over coffee. My objective for that group's session was to go into town (which held many bad memories for me from the Night of the Long Knives) and to face Jo one to one in order to see how we both felt about each other. I needed to know how we both felt; either we were still in love with each other – or we had moved apart in which case the path was clear and my heart was clear to follow a new path with Ruth I thought.

During the group I set my goal down on a piece of paper and told the rest of the group what it was (leaving out the reason why I was meeting Jo for Ruth was also in the group you understand.) I was going to meet her at 3pm, in one hour's time. As I headed out the door the group's facilitator – an Irish lady staff member – said to me "I can, I will and I'm gonna!" Words I have not forgotten to this day.

The walk down into town was a bit nerve racking but it was another beautiful day so I took it in my stride. When I had reached the outskirts of town I was early and fearful of going any further. I looked around and my eyes fell upon the city's parish church. "I've never been in there" I thought as I started to walk towards it.

Once inside I started to have a look around. Flagstones or rather tombstones adorned the church floor and crests of every sort and another adorned the walls. Whilst it was deathly quiet I somehow got the sense of peace in there as I walked around the pews. After making a full circle of the church, while stopping occasionally to read a tombstone or two, I found myself back towards the entrance again. My eyes then fell upon a prayer box with a slit in it for coins I guessed.

"Well Jeff, you surely could do with the good Lords help now. Put a quid

in the box and say a prayer...ok man here goes:...Dear Lord, you know what I've been through and you know what I have done...and I'm so very sorry for breaking your rules about Gaia and smoking weed and taking E and magic mushrooms...and I'm so very sorry for pushing Jo in the past to talk about her dead father who died in battle in the middle east...I know just because I have studied psychology doesn't make me you Lord...nor anyone else for that matter...and I'm so sorry for the trouble I have caused to both her family and mine dear Lord... but if you can see your way to making this meeting go ok – for both our sakes – then I will be eternally grateful...thank you God...Amen"

With that I dropped the pound coin into the prayer box and walked back out into the sunshine.

Soon I was standing outside the coffee shop where Jo and I had arranged to meet. "Well here goes" I thought as I stepped inside. After looking around for her on the ground no-smoking level I ordered myself a drink. After paying I went upstairs and found her sitting at the window in the smoking section.

She was wearing my favourite flowery top that she liked to wear. I smiled and sat down opposite her and rolled a cig. We chit chatted for a long time – not really getting to the point and essence of why we were meeting up. I still loved her and found her attractive but something had shifted in me. But it hadn't with her. I had moved on – my 'experience' in Hell had shifted me in a way I could not describe or can't even now. I could sense that she did not want to get back together with me but rather – just wanted to see that I was ok again. Well – I was certainly on the mend again that was for sure. Before I started to think about asking her how she felt about me I suddenly stopped myself. "Jeff – you have your answer already – don't put Jo through that unnecessarily" I thought.

With that I said I had to go. We hugged and I left her finishing her coffee and cig. I felt happy and free. My heart didn't, after all, feel the same way about Jo than it had previously, and I sensed hers didn't either. "The path is clear and so are the cobwebs now" I thought as I strolled back up to the hospital.

I then remember nearing a road crossing my side of the street. There were also traffic lights and a level crossing which was on red for pedestrians. I then, suddenly, felt an overwhelming wave of love and comfort sweep over my body in a way that's so very difficult to describe in words. This was bigger that my 'realisation' moment with the 'circle' and the episode I had dancing with Gaia and felt thousands of people.

No, this was entirely different for a number of reasons. Firstly, there was a direction from which the love and comfort came from; my top right-hand side. Secondly, I then had the impression of 'knowing' some kind of knowledge from the source of this overwhelming love. I do want to say at this point that the source had a tremendous sense of humour and acceptance – regardless of what I had done in the past. Moreover, it somehow imparted to me some kind of knowledge. Yet there were no words, in fact nothing was flowing through my mind but only pure love and acceptance. I repeat I did not hear any voice.

This 'source' then 'told' me, for the lack of a better word, that the patch of greenery that my eyes were focusing on, on the other side of the road, would be a patch of clover. Not only that – but the very first clover that came into sharp focus would be a four-leafed clover. I was a 150% sure of the source's certainty.

This held poignant significance to me because as a child I had always looked for four- leafed clovers. I would tell you what I was thinking at this stage but the truth is – I wasn't thinking of anything. I was just feeling and experiencing this overwhelming love from this benevolent 'source'.

I carried on walking and sure enough I could make out a patch of clover on the other side of the road. The crossing lights then turned green as I carried on walking. I was in a daze and I could hear nothing at this stage; not the traffic, not the birds, nothing. I crossed over the road and suddenly a single clover came into sharp focus. I was still trusting the source a 150% and had a big smile on my face.

Soon I was standing right by the patch of clovers. I bent down to take a closer look at the one clover I had been looking at all this time. I reached out my hand and picked it up. You guessed it; it was a four-leafed clover. I smiled and said a thank-you to God and carried on walking. I was beaming and my heart was filled with so much love, acceptance, happiness and laughter that I could barely contain myself.

33

Christmas Leave

Once back on the ward I immediately told Ray, Michael and Ruth about my experience and showed them the four-leafed clover. Whilst I hadn't been brought up believing in God I was surely trusting Him and thanking Him for my blessing that day. I then went into the dormitory and pressed the four-leafed clover in one of my sketch books I had been given for my birthday for safe keeping.

As the days passed I felt my heart had begun its mending process from my time with Jo and I couldn't have been happier. My feelings also seemed to grow for Ruth as we spent more and more time together. I was soon going to tell her how I felt about her and I could sense that she felt the same way about me. Michael also noticed this as he wrote the most tender and sweet poem about us and gave it to me one day shortly before I was due to have my first over-night leave home.

I was reluctant to leave the ward at this stage. Call it institution-alization or simply that I felt comfortable and protected on the ward, I don't know which. Well, I had been on the ward since the 8th of November and it was now coming up to Christmas time. But I was eager to see my Mum again and spend time with my Bro at home.

Once at home I felt the need to make amends with my surroundings, with Gaia and with God. It was difficult being home as it held many bad memories for me and reminded me of the phases and episode I had just gone through. That said, however, I was determined to put things right as best I could. "I need to make amends at both the Castle and in the lower woods at the intersection by giving an offering" I thought as I went into Mum's garden. "But what could I give?" I thought as I stood there thinking. My eyes then fell upon some rosemary growing in a pot near the patio doors. I bent down and pinched off two sprigs of it and went back inside.

Once inside I started to tie on an 'evil eye' to each of the rosemary sprigs I had taken. Mum had given me several 'evil eyes' from Turkey after her last visit there some months before I went into hospital. In Turkey, 'evil eyes' are blue and white glass objects used to ward off evil spirits. "This will be perfect" I thought as I headed out and made my way to the Castle first.

Once there I walked up to the entrance to it and laid my rosemary and 'evil eye' offering at its door. "Dear Lord, please forgive my thoughts and actions at this place" I thought. I then headed down towards the lower woods and towards the infamous path intersection. Once I was there I knelt down and carefully placed the second sprig on the ground.

"Dear Lord and Gaia, please forgive my ignorance and abuse of what you produce here in nature. Please cleanse this place with this offering and please know that I am truly sorry for what I have done to you both and my family. Amen."

The rest of the stay went well as I recall after that and I headed back to the ward on a natural high.

Before I knew it was Christmas and I was due to stay over at

Mum's again and celebrate Christmas with my family as normal; with my Mum, my Bro and I. After saying my goodbyes to my friends on the ward I headed out with Mum for home on Christmas Eve. On Christmas morning my Bro and I opened our stockings as normal and watched National Lampoon's Christmas Vacation as usual. We do have a Christmas routine at our house you understand. When we were called to the table for Christmas lunch my Bro then put on the Christmas songs and we sat down to eat. While we don't traditionally say grace at our home, I did say the Lord's Prayer in my head as we pulled the crackers and then read out the jokes. The meal, as usual, was gorgeous – each year Mum tries to outdo herself and each year my Bro and I say that it can't be beaten. This year, however, it tasted especially good I thought.

Soon it was time for the 'big ones'; our presents under the tree and before that: the Queen's speech. It was 5 to 3 and I remember getting a bit anxious about seeing the

Queen (again) after all I had been through. Before I knew it, she was on and the national anthem started playing. She then spoke about peace on Earth and about remembering the true meaning of Christmas I remember; that of celebrating the birth of Jesus Christ. She ended her speech with the usual smile and I thought "Bless you your Royal Highness – and thank you God – she didn't seem angry with me after all."

When it came time for me to leave I said "see you soon" to my Bro and left to go back to the ward. Mum drove me back there late on Christmas night as I had decided to spend some time with those 'inmates' who could not or did not leave for the day. This included both Ray and Michael.

Soon my time at St. Michael's Hospital was to come to an end. On the 10th of January 2001 I left the ward and the hospital having made a few good friends, one girlfriend in Ruth, and for the first time I truly knew what it was like to know and feel God in my life. I couldn't have been happier. I had changed; my life's direction had shifted and so had my love for Jo. But most importantly, I knew what it meant to have Faith and to love God for the first time in my entire life.

34

⟨❦⟩

The Canary

PART THREE: Back Out of the Mine

As the canary goes down the mine to help the miner and save him from a gaseous end, so the psychotic goes inside himself – down to the depths of his unconscious and the collective unconscious to help save himself and others respectfully. In other words, we sensitive souls who have a predisposition for what western psychiatrists term psychosis could be viewed as a kind of 'social canary' for the benefit of humanity and society at large. The choice is up to you and all of us how we choose to view these people and their experiences.

I remember once that my Mum, whilst training to become a psychiatric nurse, read a book about how they treat people going through 'psychosis' in Africa and she told me about it. In some African tribal cultures, she said, the psychotic works with the doctor or shaman of the tribe. The belief is that the symptoms of the psychotic individual are really symptoms of the whole community or tribe; reflecting its troubles and woes and offering a way to work with them through the individual. In short, the individual is revered as the shaman is within the tribe. I believe that families, social networks and friends and the community and society at large in the western world could learn more about themselves and their relationships if they just change their way of viewing these types of individuals. This way of viewing the social canary, I believe, can be a more useful way of viewing people undergoing these types of experiences rather than dismissing their symptoms away as 'delusions' and fantasies which are not really real in any sense and without any real meaning.

I hope that what I have demonstrated in this book and with the story of my journey is that while I did a few things to precipitate my episode (through the use of illicit drugs) the experience itself is very actually real in the true sense of the word for the individual undergoing the experience. After all – what do we mean by 'reality'? To quote the film *The Matrix* and the character Morpheus, "What do we mean by real? If real is what you can feel, smell, taste and see, then 'real' is simply electrical signals interpreted by your brain." All of my bodily senses were working (albeit possibly at heightened acuity) and therefore I perceived and sensed the reality that was unfolding before me.

What kind of reality was it however? Well, it was my reality and that is all that anyone of us has at any given point in our lives. I hope that this journey of mine has illustrated the very real phenomenon that we all, as individuals, create our own realities and no–one can tell us otherwise whilst in that state. Is it our shared, every day, 'normal' consensus reality? Not for most, no, it isn't. But does that make it any less real?

One must remember when thinking on this issue what the well-known Indian sage Krishnamurti once said, that the form of consciousness that we normally use corrupts reality:

"The ancient hope of metaphysics and physics, that thought might reveal reality, is necessarily doomed. Thought is a reactive, not an active ability, attuning man only partially to nature; distorting most of it. Thought is a

fossilised kind of consciousness, operating within 'the known' and thus by definition is uncreative." (Weber, 1982: 35)

One could argue, therefore, that every consciousness is blind to the trueness of reality as it is – not how it is formed or perceived by the individual. In order to truly 'know' reality as it is – perhaps, therefore, one must stop thinking and trying to know anything – but simply be and allow oneself to explore the unconscious and collective unconscious like I believe I did.

That having been said, what do I believe I went through? Well, I would say that I underwent a spiritual emergency and transformation. Sadly, however, the typical western psychiatry model does not recognize these types of experiences as requiring medical intervention or treatment. Spiritual and or religious experiences are now so far divorced from science and medicine in the western world that people who are experiencing these types of states are often, I believe, left without a place to go to for treatment or support or even basic simple care and understanding.

Things are changing however. The world of transpersonal psychology and psychotherapy is growing and more and more people are seeking out these types of trained individuals to help them through their spiritual crises. As Cortright (1997: 158) states in his book *Psychotherapy and Spirit,*

"Transpersonal psychology affirms this movement of spiritual seeking and places the highest value on the realisation of our spiritual nature. Spiritual experience is viewed as desirable and spiritual seeking is seen as natural, healthy, and, in the final analysis, the only truly fulfilling answer to the challenge of existence."

I have been reading on the subject of spiritual emergencies and transpersonal psychology for nearly nine years now and the more I read the more convinced I am that some form of spiritual emergency occurred for me during my episode.

Cortright (1997) describes this process of lifting the veil between normal consciousness and spiritual awareness as often being a slow and gradual one. Sometimes, however, he notes that this process is rapid and takes the person by complete surprise, as in my case. If the person has the inner resources and strength of character to assimilate it, then the transition will tend to be an uplifting, illuminating, and blissful one. If, on the other hand, this process erupts forcefully, the individual may find it so overwhelming that their normal integrative capabilities fail and their everyday psychological functioning is disturbed. Cortright (1997: 159) expands on this further, "new energies, beings, planes of experience bombard the person, resulting in confusion, fear, and [she/he] attempts to control what is going on. At this point, spiritual emergence becomes spiritual emergency."

Many forms of spiritual emergencies exist. Commonly, however, only 10 distinct categories are used ranging from episodes of unitive consciousness, renewal through return to the centre, crises of psychic opening and shamanic crises to name a few (Grof & Grof, 1989). That being said the one which most closely resembles what I went through I now believe is what Dr. David Lukoff (1985) proposed as being a Mystical Experience with Psychotic Features or MEPF.

I say this for a number of reasons but I will outline two reasons here. The first deals with ego functioning. Cortright (1997: 170) makes the distinction between psychosis and a spiritual emergency,

"Many times in spiritual emergency the person is afraid of going crazy whereas in psychosis the person is crazy and lost in the experience, that is, with little or no observing ego."

In my journey I had the ability to hold a dialogue about what was occurring for me and how I perceived my surroundings, with myself. This would demonstrate a functioning ego trying to make sense of what appeared to be a kind of organised chaos. From this mess I tried to make sense and reason answers in a form of logic based on the information I had available to me at the time. In short, I was not acting randomly in the context of what I was experiencing. Moreover, in one part of the story, I was actually very afraid of going crazy whilst I was on the ward. To have this ability to be afraid of *going* crazy demonstrates a functioning and observing ego. This would fit with the criteria for MEPF as will be outlined soon.

The second reason I feel my experience seems to fit with an MEPF is that elements of my experience seems to fit with a psychotic-like episode also. For starters I lost my memory for just over week just before going into hospital, hence I lost ego functioning during this time I believe. Secondly, I did not appear to do much reality checking in the sense of looking for rational and plausible answers and solutions in this consensus reality for what I was observing and experiencing, choosing, instead, to give in to the terror of paranoia. Lastly, I had very little insight into what was actually occurring at times due to a lack of a meaningful framework in which to work with.

Let us now look at what Lukoff (1985) describes as being the diagnostic criteria for MEPF.

DIAGNOSTIC CRITERIA FOR MEPF, (LUKOFF, 1985).

1. *Ecstatic mood.*
2. *Sense of newly gained knowledge.*
3. *Perceptual Heightening and hallucinations of the five senses.*
4. *Delusions, if present, have mythological themes. Very much in line with*

Perry's (1974) research on the mythological dimensions of psychotic process, the eight major mythological themes are:

- Death. *Being dead, meeting the dead, or meeting*
- Rebirth. *New identity or name, resurrection, apotheosis to God, king or messiah.*
- Journey. *Sense of being on a mission or journey*
- Encounters with *With either demonic or helping spirits.*
- Cosmic *Good/evil, light/dark, sun/moon, male/female.*
- Magical *Telepathy, clairvoyance, Telekinesis (ability to move objects with the mind), psychic powers.*
- New *The dawning of the New Age, rapid societal change, religion, Utopia, world peace.*
- Divine union. God as father, mother, child; marriage to God, Christ, Virgin Mary, Radha or Krishna et cetera.

5. No conceptual disorganization. (Delusional metaphoric speech may be present which is difficult to understand but is comprehensible. This metaphorical speech, which can appear to be disorganized, is not really a form of conceptual disorganization but can be understood from within the experiential world of the client in meaningful and coherent ways.)

6. Low The person is not a significant risk for homicidal or suicidal behavior.

If two of the four following criteria are satisfied, the episode is likely to have a positive outcome:

- *Good pre-episode functioning*
- *Acute onset less than three months*
- *Stressful precipitants.*
- *Positive attitude toward experience*

Let us briefly examine the criteria and see how they match with my journey. I certainly had ecstatic mood at times, and felt as though I had gained newly found knowledge. Perceptual alterations were present and I meet at least 6 out of the 8 mythological themes for the 'delusions'. One could argue that I had no conceptual disorganization as my speech in the context of my experiential world was coherent and meaningful. The only one category from the criteria that one could argue against in my case is that at one point in the journey I did, indeed, have a fleeting moment of suicidal thoughts. I doubt, however, that in a more transpersonal-orientated surrounding and with people trained in this approach that I would have had these thoughts. This would be increasingly true if they had intervened before my need to go into hospital had occurred. Lastly, I am largely positive about my experience or journey and this is illustrated by meeting two of the four criteria outlined for a positive outcome.

Obviously, the most noticeable factors for my having a very positive outcome in all of this are my realizations about and four-leafed clover 'moment' with God. Let us now examine how this canary had a helping hand from the Lord and how this has affected my view on my whole 'psychotic' or MEPF experience.

35

The Return of the Prodigal Son

Thomas Szasz once said that "If you talk to God, you are praying; If God talks to you, you have schizophrenia. If the dead talk to you, you are a spiritualist; If you talk to the dead, you are a schizophrenic." (Szasz, 1973: 113). This might indicate to the reader that I have schizophrenia. That being said, on no occasion did I ever hear a voice in the traditional sense of 'hearing voices'. Moreover, after many years of studying and working in the adult mental health field in England, and now in the USA, I would say I have become quite familiar with the symptoms of schizophrenia and I do not have many of the classical symptoms, hearing voices being one which stands out.

What I also do not really have is a basis of comparison for a mystical or divine experience. Szasz's quote above illustrates the difficulty in the modern western world when confessing to have had contact with a divine or the Divine Source or God or Krishna Consciousness or whatever name one chooses to call Him.

This unitive experience with the divine is often the pinnacle of many eastern philosophies and religions however. It is seen as a perfectly natural and healthy a pursuit and when and if it occurs one is revered or followed and not diagnosed.

Indeed, the well-known comparative religious philosopher Alan Watts once added that many of the eastern religions and philosophies actively pursue a change or shift in consciousness while western religions do not really advocate this. Moreover, he adds while typical western religions believe in the existence of the Son of God in Jesus or prophets in other religions it is frowned upon for anyone else to gain a sense in which, or even a feeling, that we too have the same or similar contact or miraculous experience with the Divine. Why is this so? This is a complex question that I leave up to you to think about.

The net result of this for us social canaries, however, is that we are diagnosed and often stigmatised. Did Jesus not say however "I am the way and the truth and the life. No one comes to the Father except through me" (The Bible, John: 14:6). In my mind does this not also mean as well as follow Jesus' teachings and manners but also His thinking and beliefs? Is it any wonder then that when one has a unitive spiritual experience like I did with God or the Source, that it's any wonder that they feel like as if they actually *are* Jesus or God Himself? I think not.

As Cortright (1997: 159) outlines below, often people undergoing spiritual emergencies or SE often have one of two contexts or conceptual frameworks from which to work with and hence three possible outcomes:

TWO CIRCUMSTANCES IN WHICH SE HAPPENS, (CORTRIGHT, 1997).

1. *The person or environment has no conceptual framework to deal with what the person is experiencing. It is then usually pathologized by the person's support system, parents, doctors, et cetera. This is relatively easy to work with. Providing a cognitive framework and supportive environment in which the person can fully experience the process is often sufficient to enable the person to assimilate what is going on.*

2. *There is not enough physical or emotional resilience within the self to integrate these experiences. Psychological structures become disorganised as the self*

THREE RESPONSES TO SE, (CORTRIGHT, 1997)

1.   *Integrate the experience, move forward in*
2.   *Be overwhelmed for a period of time, with integration*
3.   *Fixate and fail to The experience may subside, but the person remains fixated on some level, resulting in lessened or marginal adaptation.*

I would make the case that my context followed the first circumstance as outlined by Cortright. While I have been brought up in the largely Christian west, I did not really have the conceptual framework in which to assimilate the experience initially. I was pathologized by the system. That said I did after reading on this subject provide my own conceptual framework to help myself assimilate the experience.

My response to my spiritual emergency, I now feel, fell into the second category; that is I was overwhelmed by the experience for a period of time with integration following. Not only from my reading on this subject and from listening to Alan Watts and Joseph Campbell in particular I have learned to believe what the well-known mythologist Joseph Campbell once said about the difference between the psychological crack-up and the mystic: "The difference is the one who cracks up is drowning in the water in which the mystic swims" (Campbell, 1988: 13).

It should also be fairly clear that I experienced both drowning and swimming in the divine waters. These days I am learning to swim and am staying afloat. In short, I have been redeemed; I have a second chance to know God. Moreover, I have been baptized by a great minister called Andrew and while I regret the heartache and worry I have caused my family and friends, I do not regret having gone through my experience. I have found God and it is with His love I move forward in my life.

In conclusion, I now believe that acute 'madness', while being partly what Thomas Szasz calls a socially constructed phenomenon due to it being uncomfortable with us spiritual and social canaries calling themselves Jesus or God, is also a stage of conscious and unconscious conflict typically containing pain, suffering and searching, endured by the soul which just proceeds the potential for greater self-realization. This potential stage is part of a journey characterized by an inherent, unconscious and divine drive towards individuation and greater conscious acceptance of Self; the true Self – which is at one with God.

36

⚜

Final Thoughts

Whilst my experience, I am pleased to say, had a very positive outcome I would like to take this opportunity to propose a few thoughts to a number of groups of people; to young adults, to other spiritual and social canaries, to families and carers and to mental health professionals.

For Young Adults

If you are anything like I was at your age then you might be thinking that you would like to explore your own mind and consciousness. Having a sense of identity is also very important at this stage of your life and you might be thinking of ways in which to explore it. You can do this by changing your style of clothes or hair, or by what music you listen to. All of this is important but how might you go about exploring the core element of your identity; your mind and consciousness?

I know that illicit drugs are rife in our country at the moment and you might know someone who might be able to get you some. You may even know someone that has tried some and they seem to be fine smoking it or taking it. They have a good time dancing or laughing and it appears to have the desired effect. However, it's a game of chance. By this I mean I had no way of telling that it was going to affect me the way it did and send me into the state I describe in my story. One week I was fine and the next I wasn't.

I'm not merely talking about a 'bad trip' but something potentially much much worse. I was lucky enough to come out of the mine, but my time spent down there I would not wish on my worst enemy. The fear and paranoia is so intense that it almost made me commit suicide. What if I had really done that? How would my family and friends have felt if I had succeeded? And what, Heaven forbid, if I stayed in Hell all my life? My Mum, who trained as a psychiatric nurse, was very fearful of me staying catatonic for the rest of my life – especially when I wasn't talking. Think about it – is it worth getting high when you could be in Hell for the rest of your life?

FRANK, the online website about illicit drugs, lists some of the risks of smoking cannabis alone as being:

- Even hardcore smokers can become anxious, panicky, suspicious or
- Cannabis affects your coordination, which is one of the reasons why drug driving is just as illegal as drink driving.
- Some people think cannabis is harmless just because it's a plant – but it isn't Cannabis, like tobacco, has lots of chemical 'nasties', which can cause lung disease and possibly cancer with long-term or heavy use, especially as it is often mixed with tobacco and smoked without a filter. It can also make asthma worse, and cause wheezing in non-asthma sufferers.
- Cannabis itself can affect many different systems in the body,

including the heart: It increases the heart rate and can affect blood pressure.

- If you've a history of mental health problems, then taking cannabis is not a good idea: It can cause paranoia in the short term, but in those with a pre-existing psychotic illness, such as schizophrenia, it can contribute to relapse.
- If you use cannabis and have a family background of mental illness, such as schizophrenia, you may be at increased risk of developing a psychotic illness.
- It is reported that frequent use of cannabis can cut a man's sperm count, reduce sperm motility, and can suppress ovulation in women and so may affect fertility.
- If you're pregnant, smoking cannabis frequently may have some association with the risk of the baby being born smaller than expected.
- Regular, heavy use makes it difficult to learn and concentrate. Some people begin to feel tired all the time and can't seem to get motivated.
- Some users may want to buy strong herbal cannabis to get 'a bigger high' but unpleasant reactions can be more powerful when you use strong cannabis, and it is possible that using strong cannabis repeatedly could lead in time to more users experiencing harmful effects such as dependence or being more at risk of developing the mental health effects.

To find out more information about cannabis or other illicit drugs please visit the FRANK website at: http://www.talktofrank.com

I have seen first-hand and second hand through my work, the nasty effect that cannabis use in particular can have on people's minds and behaviour. But don't just take my word for it, do your own research and you will see that cannabis use is being increasingly linked to long-term mental health problems and to psychosis-related conditions in particular more and more. Why else has it been re-classified by the government from a class C drug to a class B drug now? Think about it.

Ok that's the warning out the way. So, you are probably left thinking what might I have done differently, instead of doing drugs, to find myself and explore my mind and consciousness? Well, for starters, I would have carried on with my poetry and writings. I now paint a lot and I would have explored my unconscious through this way. I might also have taken up a form of martial art – like I did after coming out of hospital – I did Tai Chi – but there are many other good forms out there. Meditation is another good form of exploring yourself from the inside out. Perhaps find a local meditation class in your area.

Lastly, I would have read a lot and listen to such people as Alan Watts (for those of you who are interested in eastern and western philosophies and religions) for example. Listen to people you respect and have something meaningful to say that resonates with you. There are many other great thinkers out there in this world, some I dare say, who have tried drugs, but you don't have to. They have done the hard work for you and now you can read about their experiences, thoughts and theories, without the risk, just like you have done with my story.

For The Spiritual and Social Canaries

While some early intervention services for young people experiencing their first episode of 'psychosis' do exist in England, these services might not be an option for you (if you live abroad or you live in an area where they currently do not have one) or you might find that they have become involved in your care too late to stop you going through an acute phase of your journey or episode. If you are able to contact one of these services, however, I would recommend that you do so, perhaps with the help of your family or carer. I would recommend calling NHS Direct (0845 4647) for help and assistance on finding one of these services in England.

What if this is not an option for you however? If you are able to read this and make sense of it then I would say that you have a good chance to positively affect the outcome of your episode. DO seek some kind of help. Seeking help does not necessarily mean that you will need to go into hospital. In some cases, people can be successfully cared for and supported through their episode whilst at home or at some kind of day unit or day hospital. Contact your local mental health provider or ask someone to do it for you.

I hope that my story has illustrated to you that it does not mean that what you are going through means that you are in any way 'mad' or 'crazy'. Depending on what you experience and how you think about it, it may just mean that you need a supportive and safe place to explore the shift in consciousness that you are experiencing.

DO try and communicate with others (be it with family or carers or mental health professionals.) I know that it can be a very daunting thing to do but the more you are able to communicate to others what you are experiencing the better they will be to be able to help you. Obviously choosing people who are sympathetic to your kind of experience will help matters. Think carefully about what kind of episode or change in consciousness you are undergoing and then seek out those professional people in the field that might be able to help you. Remember – they are there to help you – they are not against you.

If you are not able to talk, DO write down your thoughts and experiences – or if you can't write – doodle, paint or sculpt them. Do whatever it takes to create some kind of expressional form from them. This will not only help others understand you but it might also help you better internalize and assimilate and make sense of what is happening to you, if not now but maybe in the future. Who knows, you might end up writing a book like this to help others.

What about medication and drugs? Well, if you are or have been taking any kind of illicit drugs, stop doing them NOW. As for medication, that is a subject which I cannot advise you on as I am not a trained doctor or psychiatric nurse. I can say, however, they might be able to help you if your episode is going badly in some way. Do consider them and seek further advice from a trained professional about them as many different anti- psychotics exist out there.

If, however, you are coming out of an episode and are reading this, then there a number of things you could be doing now which will help you and others in the future should this ever happen again. First, make a list of your early warning signs. By this I mean, what were the first signs that you were experiencing that shift of consciousness? Things that are on my list include (so as to give you some examples): 1) Drinking black coffee in excess, 2) Having nightmares, 3) Feeling like I was on a mission and 4) Everything seemed to fall into extremes.

Next, write what I have called your 'very good steps to take'. This document outlines what you did while you were beginning to go through your episode or change in consciousness that helped you. Mental health professionals might call this your relapse prevention plan or other similar thing. It doesn't matter what you call it, just try and write one. In this try and think about all the things that helped you whilst you were going through your episode, like, for example, avoiding drinking alcohol and maybe spending time around others.

In the final document you can write the things that didn't help you. Call it whatever you want but typically these things are included into what's called an advanced statement or directive. Should you lose ego functioning and/or insight into your condition or shift in consciousness then what are the things that wouldn't help you with it and what things you need in order to go through it again alright and safely. For example, in mine I state that wearing black clothes around me is a big no-no and trying to keep me in doors would help me. Not having ECT is also included in mine.

While there are several 'official' templates out there on the web for doing these you don't have to use them if you don't want to. One such thing which incorporates a number of these documents is called the WRAP or Wellness Recovery Action Plan. It is a rather lengthy document but it might be helpful to some of you.

Ok, so you have written these documents – what then? Well, keep a copy of them yourself in a safe place that is easy to find. Secondly, give a copy of them to your partner, family member or carer. This is important should you lose insight. Finally, give a copy of them to the Crisis Team in your area. Once they are on their system it should be made available to any mental health professional that works with you.

I want to leave you, my fellow canary, with a final thought and I wish you all the best for the future:

You are a canary; not a psycho. You are a canary; not a schizo. You are a canary; a sensitive soul who experiences shifts in consciousness. Full-stop. Don't define who you are and your entire being with a label. If I ate a steak once in my life or even twice, would you say that I am a steak lover? No of course not. Don't do the same with stigmatizing and unhelpful labels. You are much more than that – and you know it.

For Families, Carers and Mental Health Professionals

First of all, I want to address families and carers. The first thing to mention is that while your family member or friend might seem to be going through a state of 'madness' or delusional state, it is nevertheless very actually real for them. Refrain from calling them labels of this type as ultimately it won't help the situation. Moreover, who are we to judge what someone is going through isn't reality in one sense or another? Many people in the world of theoretical physics are currently working on what's called the M-Theory of everything in which they propose 11 dimensions of space-time. Look this up on Google. There may be more to this universe than simply the 'reality' that you live in.

The reason I mention this is because to challenge your family member's behaviour or speech would not only be degrading to their experiences but also pointless, especially if they have lost the capacity for insight. Even if they haven't, one must remember that this 'reality' or change in consciousness is very real for them. Therefore, in short, it is, by all intense and purposes, very actually 'real'; as real as your 'reality'. So please, treat them with respect and resist the temptation to tell them to 'snap out of it' or other similar request. They simply can't.

So what can you do to help? Well you can do a lot, is the short answer. The longer answer is that you can find ways to help them go through their episode as safely and as calmly as possible. Firstly, try and get them to talk about their experiences. The more informed you are the better equipped you will be to direct them to someone who might be able to help them. Next, do some research. From what you have learnt see if you can find other family members or carers in a similar situation. Also, you may want to contact your local mental health service for they may have a carer's support network.

Do try and get the appropriate help based on the research you have found. It's hard to say at this point what services you should go with but use your judgement for this. Ask the person in question and consult them in this process – they might be able to help you.

Do trust the mental health professionals. While I know you know the person in question more than they do the mental health professional also has experience working with these types of individuals undergoing this type of experience – if you have directed them to the appropriate person or place. Make sure they listen to you and take your information and advice about the person seriously. After all – you know them better than they do. Lastly, be a part of their care plan, and in this country, make sure you are included (if the person wants) in their CPA or Care Program Approach process and meetings. Stay strong, positive and loving throughout their experience; it's worth its weight in gold.

I now want to turn my attention to the mental health professional. As I have said above, do include the person's support network and or parents and family in the person's care. They are a valuable source of information. Also, it would help if you familiarize yourself with the world of transpersonal psychology as I have done. I believe it is the way of the future for psychiatry; if you haven't done so, or do not have the time to, then consult your Trust's spiritual and pastoral service for advice or your service's chaplaincy. When visiting a person undergoing these types of experiences it would be helpful if the spiritual person wears lay clothes I would suggest.

Treat the person with respect and dignity. I know this might be a given for most professionals but sadly however, some get through the gates that choose to employ the old way of treating 'patients' or service users as crazy people. This is an outdated, unhelpful and degrading form of treatment. They are just as human as you are.

Please check if they have advance statements or directives. Ask their carer or family member for one if they do not give you one. This is becoming increasingly standardized in this country and, I hope, in your country also.

Lastly, please ensure that service user involvement is not lost within your service. If regular community meetings with service users are not happening, propose that they do with your manager. Include service users in all aspects of service care and delivery and improvement at every level. We hold the necessary feedback you need to make your service better. Don't marginalize us by saying or thinking – oh there goes another psycho or schizo – change your attitude and others' attitudes by your own actions. Be a role model in your service and shine for us canaries.

I am privileged to have worked in a service with staff members who respect and value us canaries. They followed all of the above and I hope that you, like they do, shine as beacons of hope and recovery for suffering canaries in times of need. Bless you and the work you do.

References

- Campbell, J. (1988). *The power of myth*. New York: Broadway Books.
- Cortright, B. (1997). *Psychotherapy and spirit*. Albany, NY: State University of New York Press.
- Grof, S., & Grof, C. (1989). (Eds.) *Spiritual emergency: When personal transformation becomes a crisis*. Los Angeles: Tarcher.
- Lukoff, D. (1985). *Diagnosis of mystical experiences with psychotic features*. Journal of Transpersonal Psychology, Vol. 17 (No. 2), 155-181.
- Szasz, T. S. (1973). *The second sin*. Garden City, NY: Anchor/Doubleday.
- Weber, R. (1982). Field consciousness and field ethics. In K. Wilber (Ed.), *The holographic paradigm and other paradoxes*. London: New Science Library.

www.ingramcontent.com/pod-product-compliance
Lightning Source LLC
Chambersburg PA
CBHW060527130626
46553CB00002B/671